REVEALING THE HEART OF PRAYER

THE GOSPEL OF LUKE

**Other titles in
the Transformative Word series:**

When You Want to Yell at God: The Book of Job
by Craig G. Bartholomew

God Behind the Scenes: The Book of Esther
by Wayne K. Barkhuizen

Faith Amid the Ruins: The Book of Habakkuk
by Heath A. Thomas

Together for the World: The Book of Acts
by Michael R. Wagenman

Cutting Ties with Darkness: 2 Corinthians
by John D. Barry

Between the Cross and the Throne: The Book of Revelation
by Matthew Y. Emerson

REVEALING THE HEART OF PRAYER

THE GOSPEL OF LUKE

TRANSFORMATIVE WORD

CRAIG G. BARTHOLOMEW

Author and Series Editor

LEXHAM PRESS

Revealing the Heart of Prayer: The Gospel of Luke
Transformative Word

Copyright 2016 Craig G. Bartholomew

Lexham Press, 1313 Commercial St., Bellingham, WA 98225
LexhamPress.com

Print ISBN 9781577997153
Digital ISBN 9781577997160

Series Editor: Craig G. Bartholomew
Lexham Editorial: Donna Huisjen, Abby Salinger, Lynnea Smoyer,
    Abigail Stocker, Elizabeth Vince
Cover Design: Brittany Schrock
Back Cover Design: Liz Donovan
Typesetting: ProjectLuz.com

TABLE OF CONTENTS

1. Introduction 1

2. The Gospel of Luke as the Story of Jesus 7

3. The Centrality of Prayer in Jesus'
   Life and Ministry 23

4. Prayer and the Story of Redemption in Luke 35

5. The Acts of the Apostles—Part 2 43

6. Prayer and Reading Luke 49

7. Prayer and Full-Time Ministry 59

8. Why Prayer Must Be Central 65

9. Jesus' Practice of Prayer 71

10. Prayer and Ministry 81

11. Praying Continually 87

Resources for Further Reading 89

Notes 91

INTRODUCTION

Fires ordinarily blaze in the open, but not so with prayer. Prayer is like a hidden fire whose effects are seen in our humanity and in God's response. We are made for God, and thus there is nothing more human than prayer—that open stance in relation to the living God who has come to us in Jesus. However, on the basis of its hiddenness, we easily neglect prayer and settle for less when God wants to give us so much more of himself. The following story comes from the Desert Fathers (early Christian hermits and monks who lived mostly in the deserts of Egypt):

> Abba Lot went to see Abba Joseph and said to him, "Abba, as far as I can I say my Little Office. I fast a little. I pray. I meditate. I live in peace and as far as I can I purify my thoughts. What else am I to do?" "What else," Abba Lot says, "can I do?" Then the old man stood up, stretched his hands towards heaven and his fingers became like ten lamps of fire, and he said to him, "If you will, you can become all flame."[1]

OUTLINE OF THE GOSPEL OF LUKE

Luke 1:1–4—The prologue: Luke's purpose for writing

Luke 1:5–9:50—The unique identity of Jesus: God's agent of salvation

Luke 1:5–2:52—Infancy narratives: Jesus' unique birth

Luke 3:1–4:13—Preparation for ministry: Jesus' unique ministry qualifications

Luke 4:14–9:50—Early ministry: Jesus' unique power and authority

Luke 9:51–24:53—The unique mission of Jesus: leading the people of faith

Luke 9:51–19:27—Travel narrative: reordered priorities for following Jesus

Luke 19:28–23:53—Jesus in Jerusalem: Jesus' handling of conflict

Luke 24:1–53—The resurrection and ascension: Jesus' victory and exaltation[2]

As disciples, we are followers of Jesus. In this book we will explore Luke's Gospel through the theme of prayer, with a particular focus on what we can learn about prayer from Jesus himself. I encourage you to work slowly and prayerfully through this volume, with Luke's Gospel constantly at hand. Here is a prayer for you to pray now and to return to throughout the course of our journey together:

Lord, open my eyes to see Jesus,
    his greatness, his grace, his humility.
Let your Spirit illumine him,

so that I might see him
and become like him,
living in communion with you,
all flame.
Amen.

Jesus, the Incarnate One

The four Gospels, including Luke, all tell the story of
the incarnation in one way or another. Athanasius, in
his classic *On the Incarnation*, perceptively notes that
in order to understand the incarnation—and thus
Luke's Gospel—we need to first understand creation
and what it means to be human, to be created in the
image of God:

> We should not think that the Savior has
> worn a body as a consequence of nature, but
> that, being by nature bodiless and existing
> as the Word, by the love for humankind and
> goodness of his own Father he appeared to
> us in a human body for our salvation. As we
> give an account of this, it is first necessary
> to speak about the creation of the universe
> and its maker, God, so that one may thus
> worthily reflect that its recreation was ac-
> complished by the Word who created it in
> the beginning. For it will appear not at all
> contradictory if the Father works its salva-
> tion in the same one by whom he created it.[4]

We will, as Athanasius points out, misunderstand
the incarnation and story of Jesus if we fail to note how
they fit into the context of the grand, overarching story of the Bible. Luke alerts us to this in his genealogy

of Jesus (3:23-37), which he delineates at the outset of Jesus' public ministry to eliminate any question about who Jesus is. Through the line of Joseph, Luke traces Jesus' genealogy backward through David, Abraham, and Noah all the way back to Adam, "the son of God." Matthew, by contrast, starts with Abraham and draws attention to Jesus as the son of Abraham, the son of David (Matt 1:1-17). Luke's unique approach in drawing our attention to Jesus as the son of Adam ensures that we connect his public ministry with God's purposes for his entire creation. Using Paul's language (see Rom 5:15), Luke alerts us that Jesus is the "second Adam."

WORTHWHILE OLDIE?

In his preface to Saint Athanasius' *On the Incarnation*, C. S. Lewis advises, "It is a good rule, after reading a new book, never to allow yourself another new one till you have read an old one in between."[3] Athanasius (AD 296/8–373), the 20th bishop of Alexandria, wrote many works. Of the "old" books, Lewis rightly regards Athanasius' *On the Incarnation* as a classic.

Through Jesus, God is at work recovering his purposes for the whole of his creation and reversing the effect of original sin; while this certainly includes our personal salvation, there is far more to Jesus' becoming flesh than this. Athanasius evokes the enormity of what God did in Jesus' life and death by likening his arrival to that of a great king entering some large city and dwelling in one of its houses. That city, he notes, is made worthy of high honor; the king's residence wards off the very presence of evil.[5] "If a king constructed a house or a city," he goes on to observe, "and it is attacked by bandits because of the carelessness of its inhabitants, he in no way abandons it, but avenges and saves it as his own work, having regard not for the carelessness of the inhabitants but for his own honor."[6]

Jesus' incarnation and work of redemption are thus far more momentous than we might imagine. In Mary's Song (1:46-55)—commonly known as the Magnificat—Mary, in response to Elizabeth's pregnancy, refers to God's promise made "to Abraham and his descendants" (1:55). This takes us right back to Genesis 12:1-3, in which God promises that through Abraham and his descendants God will reverse the effect of judgment on creation and bring blessing instead. In Jesus, the Father is at work recovering his purpose of blessing for his entire creation, so it is fitting that we approach Luke's Gospel with a sense of expectancy and awe. As the incarnate one, Jesus is clearly portrayed in Luke's Gospel as the second Adam, who not only redeems our humanity but also shows us what true humanity looks like. In Genesis 3:8 we read by implication how God would walk with Adam and Eve in Eden, which teaches us that communion with God is one of his primary purposes in creating us. Prayer is thus the quintessentially human act; not surprisingly, Luke portrays Jesus, the second Adam, as a man of prayer. If we wish to become like Jesus, and thus fully human, we will need to attend closely to Jesus' teaching and example when it comes to prayer.

| **SUGGESTED READING**
☐   John 1:1–14

Reflection

What does the word "incarnation" mean to you?

_____

_____

_____

Select either Matthew, Luke, or John and explain how the Gospel of your choice tells the story of the incarnation. Why is it essential to understand the incarnation in the context of the biblical story as a whole?

_____

_____

_____

_____

How, in your view, is the incarnation connected with prayer?

_____

_____

_____

THE GOSPEL OF LUKE AS THE STORY OF JESUS

A cardinal rule for when we interpret the Bible is to pay attention at all times to the type of literature we are reading. Thus, we must ask what literary genre the Gospel of Luke represents. Scholars have debated at length whether the Gospels are biographies. They are clearly not biographies in the modern sense of the term, since they focus on Jesus' public ministry, and especially on his death and resurrection. To understand Luke's Gospel, we must recognize that the book is a *narrative*—a story, account, or chronicle. In this case, it is a narrative of actual, historical events. Luke himself categorizes his work as "an orderly account." He speaks of using history to preach—in this case, to set forth a persuasive proclamation of God's work in Jesus and the early church. As Joel B. Green points out, *"The medium of that proclamation is the narrative account, whose 'order' is crucial for our understanding of that interpretation."*[1] This may seem obvious, but its implications touch upon an area in which recent scholarship has made real progress.

That Luke is a narrative alerts us to the following elements, which are significant for its interpretation: characters, plot, sequencing, beginnings and endings, and narrative frames.[2] As is typical of the Gospel writers, Luke draws little attention to his own voice as narrator.[3] Thus, it is by approaching the book of Luke as narrative or story that we hear its message. Luke is also different from the other Gospels in that the author wrote a sequel: Acts of the Apostles. Luke was the doctor companion of Paul and is mentioned in several of Paul's letters (Col 4:14; 2 Tim 4:11; Phlm 1:24). As Luke recalls at the beginning of Acts, "In my former book, Theophilus, I wrote about all that Jesus began to do and teach until the day he was taken up to heaven" (Acts 1:1). In Acts, then, Luke writes about all that Jesus continues to do through the Spirit and the Church now that he is ascended to the right hand of the Father.

Again, the description of the Gospel of Luke as a story or narrative does not imply that the material is not historical. In narrative format, Luke presents for us a world in which God, Jesus, and the Spirit sent by Jesus in Acts are the main actors. The validity of this depiction depends upon the events recorded having happened in time and space,[4] but it is through narrative that these events are interpreted and a world opened up that we are invited to explore and inhabit. In cultures in which oral tradition played a large part, narrative was the principal means by which knowledge was communicated.

In this volume we will first concentrate on the story of Luke's Gospel as a whole and then hone in on

Jesus and prayer, a theme and coupling that Luke emphasizes repeatedly.

> ### LISTENING TO LUKE TELL THE STORY OF JESUS
>
> Because the Gospel of Luke is a narrative—a telling of the story of Jesus—we need to listen to it as such, being attentive as far as possible to how first-century Christians would have heard and understood Luke's words.

A. The Prologue: Luke's Purpose for Writing (Luke 1:1-4)

The prologue in Luke 1:1-4 identifies the book's type of writing, positions Luke's work among similar narratives, and alerts us to the origins of this author's narrative in eyewitness testimony. It also informs us of Luke's decision to write a similar narrative,[5] on the basis of his own careful investigation, for Theophilus, so that this recipient may "know the truth" concerning the things in which he has been instructed. A key difference between Luke and the other Gospels seems to be the intended audience: the "most excellent[6] Theophilus" and his circle of friends, whom such a dedication would have included. We know little about Theophilus, but the clearly Hellenistic style of the prologue and the man's public status point us to the Gentile character of Luke's Gospel.

There is an apologetic character to this Gospel—not in the sense of an acknowledgment of fault or failure, as "apologetic" sometimes infers, but in that

Luke offers it as a defense or vindication. Luke wants to show that the story of Jesus is the answer to the existential problems and issues facing the Graeco-Roman (Gentile) world, as well as the Jewish one. Hence the Hellenistic style—unique among the four biblical Gospels—of the prologue and Luke's particular recounting of the story as tailored for his intended audience.

The beginning and ending are important elements in every narrative. Thus, it appears necessary to decide whether Luke's account ends in Acts 28 or in Luke 24. Green notes that the "narrative unity of Luke-Acts has important implications for our reading of Luke's work. Most significantly, it requires that our understanding of the need(s) and audience he addressed account *for all the evidence*, both the Gospel and Acts."[7] This is undoubtedly true, even though in the biblical canon Luke has been separated from Acts as part of a "fourfold Gospel" collection that arose very early in the history of the Church. In my view, we need both to read Luke as a coherent whole and as the first in a two-part work. The endings of Luke *and* of Acts are significant for Luke. The action begins and ends in the temple, with the disciples continually meeting there, blessing God. Indeed, Jerusalem is central to Luke's Gospel. The prologue alerts us to the significance of the gospel (the good news of Jesus Christ) for the Roman world, and it is noteworthy that Acts ends with Paul's proclaiming the kingdom of God in Rome and teaching freely about Jesus Christ.

Although Luke's Gospel begins with the prologue, the action commences in Luke 1:5. Green notes that "Luke's prologue (1:1–4) is external to the narrative per se"[8] and that the transition to the action is abrupt. However, as both Tom Wright and Joel Green note, this shift from the world of Hellenistic history writing to the world of small-town Jewish folk is significant: "The intersection of these two worlds is of critical importance for Luke, who will show through his orderly account how the unfolding events in this world of ancient Galilee and Judaea are of universal significance."[9] In Greek, the style of language also changes from the balanced, complex prologue to a more plodding style filled with Semitisms.

B. Infancy Narratives: Jesus' Unique Birth (Luke 1:5–2:52)

The geographical and historical notes in Luke 1:5 and 3:1 demarcate this section, as does the summary in Luke 2:52. So too does the content dealing with the births of John and Jesus. It contains numerous markers—chronological, geographical, geopolitical, and topographical—all aimed at evoking dramatic narrative movement and a concrete sense of the events taking place, as well as a powerful indication of God at work in the midst of the events.

John and Jesus are the central human characters introduced in this section. Unlike his fellow chroniclers Mark and John, Luke tells us at length about the events surrounding these two pivotal births, believing rightly that these birth narratives

> From the outset, the question of how the promise implicit in Israel's story is to be fulfilled is front and center, heightening expectation as to how the narrative will unfold.

provide important clues to the mission of Jesus. Most of the material in this section is unique to Luke, and thus Johnson notes that "these chapters, are, therefore, like Acts, of particular importance in showing the reader how Luke intended his story to be understood."[10] Indeed, all the seeds of the narrative that follows are planted in this section. Parallels are clearly drawn between John and Jesus,[11] although more text is devoted to the birth of Jesus, who is clearly designated to be *the one*.[12] Both births are described as "gospel" or "good news" (1:19; 2:10),[13] closely linking John and his ministry to Jesus and his own from the outset.

In addition to the parallels between John and Jesus, the theme of connected promise, fulfilment, and praise response is repeated in the cases of Zechariah, Mary, and Simeon, whose three "songs" or prayers of praise unite the section. The roles played by Zechariah, Mary, and Simeon thus position the two births within the context of Israel's grand story. In the spirit and power of the great prophet Elijah, John will prepare a people for the Lord (1:17). Gabriel announces to Mary that her son will also be the Son of the Most High, who will be given the throne of David. The three songs anchor the births clearly within Israel's story and indicate that the God of Israel, the major actor in this section, is moving to fulfill his purposes in history. This is confirmed by the many references and allusions to the Old Testament in this section in relation to Genesis 11–21, 27–43, Daniel 7–10, etc. These references and allusions are so prevalent that Green describes this portion of Luke's narrative as an echo chamber of Old Testament texts.

Undoubtedly this section would have connected with the messianism of the day, and it is intriguing to compare the three songs in this respect. Zechariah's song reflects a strong emphasis on God delivering Israel from its enemies, whereas Simeon's song is more attentive to the equivocal response Jesus would evoke in Israel.[14] J. Massyngberde Ford argues evocatively that Luke intentionally heightens messianic expectations in this section—in particular those of the Zealots, who argued for the use of force to overthrow Roman rule, inviting contrast with Jesus' approach in the rest of the Gospel. From the outset, the question of how the promise implicit in Israel's story is to be fulfilled is front and center, heightening expectation as to how the narrative will unfold.

This section anticipates the forthcoming narrative in many ways. In this material, which is unique to Luke, we are often given access to information of which later characters will be unaware, as is often the case in biblical narrative (compare Job 1). We are invited, like Mary, to reflect upon the epochal events as they unfold. In Luke 1:66 we read that all who heard about the circumstances of John's birth "pondered them," and in Luke 2:19 (see also 2:51) we are told that Mary "treasured all these words and pondered them in her heart." Such musing is at the heart of prayerful reflection, and at these points Luke invites his readers to similarly slow down, reflect, and live contemplatively within the events.

C. Preparation for Ministry: Jesus' Unique Ministry Qualifications (Luke 3:1-4:13)

In this section we leap ahead to the commencement of John's and Jesus' public ministries. Sections B, C, and D of Luke (following the progression of this chapter's subheadings) constitute three beginnings, each of which connects to what precedes. In section B we have seen the births of John and Jesus, which are clearly flagged as the opener in God's climactic act in history. Here in section C we consider Jesus' transition from a private to a public figure—another beginning. And in section D we will consider the beginning of Jesus' public ministry.

Once again, God is the main actor: In Luke 3:2 John's public ministry is initiated in true prophetic fashion by the word of God coming to him; John's identity as the "son of Zechariah" connects this beginning back to section B. Section C also establishes the radically different identities of John and Jesus. John, the messenger of Isaiah 40:3, prepares the way of the Lord, while Jesus, the coming one, is the more powerful. Jesus' baptism is highly significant, with God himself affirming Jesus audibly as "my Son," even as Jesus identifies himself with sinners in the waters of baptism. This alerts the perceptive reader that the nature of Jesus' Sonship will be radically different from what we might have expected. "Thus," as Green points out, "we are reminded that, though the narrative spotlight turns first on John [and] then on Jesus, this is not their story. God is the primary actor around whose purpose the narrative develops."[15]

D. Early Ministry: Jesus' Unique Power and Authority (Luke 4:14-9:50)

There is no clear narrative structure in this section, consisting as it does of complex, interactive cycles. Jesus' ministry consists of both teaching and miracles, and responses to his work vary. For those who receive him there is significant instruction about discipleship. Narrative summaries, made necessary by the episodic character of the section, are found in Luke 4:14-15, 44; 5:15; 7:17; and 18:1-3.

As with beginnings in general, the onset of Jesus' public ministry in Luke 4:16-20 is bursting with meaning in terms of the ongoing story. It prefaces Jesus' entire ministry and functions as a condensed version of the gospel story as a whole; its programmatic function has been compared to that of the Sermon on the Mount in Matthew 5-7. Clearly Jesus is claiming to be the Messiah, the Servant of Isaiah 61, who is anointed by the Spirit and sent to bring liberty. Intriguingly, Jesus halts his reading from Isaiah just prior to "the day of the LORD's vengeance"; it was probably this that enraged his audience, who were hoping for a messiah who would destroy Israel's temporal enemies.

Jesus' reading, along with his strategically halting where he did, penetrate to the very heart of what Israel's story is all about and how the Gentiles fit into it. Jesus is implicitly declaring himself to be radically different from the Messiah the Jewish people expected. As the Anointed One, he will announce a Jubilee for both the Jews and their opponents. The liberty he brings is not in the service of a narrow Jewish nationalism but is creation-wide. As Johannes Nissen notes, by this means Jesus challenged the congregation's "ethics of election."[16] Indeed, Jesus' Nazareth Manifesto generated severe conflict (4:20–30)—a theme that rises to a crescendo as Luke's narrative unfolds. Here we see the cause of the opposition: a developing awareness of the true nature of the climax of Israel's story. As David Bosch notes, "The Nazareth pericope thus sets the stage for Jesus' entire ministry."[17]

E. The Unique Mission of Jesus: Leading the People of Faith (Luke 9:51–24:53)

In Luke 9 we read of Peter's confession that Jesus is the Messiah (9:18–20) and of the confirmation of this in Jesus's transfiguration (9:28–36). Typically, the disciples fail to understand that Jesus' messiahship will emerge via the cross (9:43–50).

In the opening of this next major section, Luke tells us that Jesus resolutely set out for Jerusalem. Indeed, his journey frames most of the remainder of Luke's Gospel.

F. Travel Narrative (Luke 9:51–19:27)

Luke's Gospel is exceptional in terms of the lengthy travel narrative that dominates the middle of the book, clearly marked with notes along the way. The historicity of the journey is debated; however, there is no reason to suspect that literary license and historicity conflict at this point. Either way, the journey is highly metaphorical: Jesus' unavoidable journey before he is "taken up" is replete with instruction for his disciples on "the way," and this includes teaching on prayer.

As pointed out by Kenneth E. Bailey, "The repetition of Jerusalem on the outside and at the center gives [this Gospel] a prominence that is unmistake-able."[18] The precise ending point of the narrative is unclear, however, since "for him to be taken up" in Luke 9:51 is not fulfilled until Luke 24:51. Jesus' triumphal entry into Jerusalem and his cleansing of the temple appear to mark the conclusion of his journey to Jerusalem. Luke unequivocally alerts us to the centrality of Jerusalem and makes clear that it was no mistake that Jesus arrived there at around the time of the Passover. The events to follow are no accident either, but are central to Jesus' ministry and the fulfilment of Israel's story.

A central theme in this section is the opposition to Jesus and the emphasis that the Son of Man (see Dan 7:13–14) must suffer and die (9:22, 44). This section explains how Israel's rejection of Jesus has come about: The Samaritans reject him because he is going to Jerusalem (9:51–55); some accuse him of being possessed (11:14–23); his critique of scribes and Pharisees heightens the opposition (11:37–54); he explains that he will cause deep division (12:49–53); he is told that Herod wants to kill him but insists that it is impossible for a prophet to be killed outside Jerusalem (13:31–35); and, finally, he enters Jerusalem triumphantly, though his cleansing of the temple calls forth dangerous opposition as the chief priests, scribes, and other religious leaders look for a way to kill him (20:45–48).

Essentially, it is Jesus' teaching and practices that evoke opposition. The story of Zacchaeus is instructive in this respect (19:1–10). Jesus' acceptance of Zacchaeus' hospitality arouses criticism, but Jesus insists that "the Son of Man came to seek and save the lost" (19:10).

It is in this section—in Luke 10:38–11:13 and in 18:1–14—that we find Jesus' teaching on prayer. Not surprising, in light of the growing opposition to Jesus, perseverance is a major emphasis in his teaching on the subject.

G. Jesus in Jerusalem (Luke 19:28–23:53)

Luke 20:1 and 21:37–8 provide an inclusio, a cohesive section bookended by opening and closing verses. In this case, the inclusio centers on Jesus' continual teaching in the temple. If we wonder why it was so important for Jesus to head to Jerusalem at this strategic juncture, we find the answer here, in his Father's house. "The reasoning of this narrative segment," explains Green, "proceeds on the basis of this common understanding of the essential prominence of the temple as sacred space that establishes the order of the world and provides the axial point around which social life is aligned."[19] The chief priests and scribes rightly recognize the question of authority at the heart of the matter (20:2). The temple is the microcosm representing the macrocosm of creation; if salvation—the central theme of Luke's Gospel—is to come into play, it must come here, where God dwells amid his people.

> If salvation—the central theme of Luke's Gospel—is to come into play, it must come here, where God dwells amid his people.

It is precisely here that we find the parable of the wicked tenants (20:9–19); it is not difficult to see how this penetrates to the heart of the matter or how provocative such teaching would have been in this context; the same is true of Jesus' prophecy of the destruction of the temple (21:5–6).

The theme of conflict comes to a literal climax in Luke 22:1–23:56. The timing is highly significant in that the Feast of Unleavened Bread and the Passover enact the drama of Israel's identity—the very question that lies at the heart of Jesus' ministry and that is evoking such opposition. In this section of Luke's Gospel the people provide a buffer between Jesus and his opponents, but this buffer is porous, and as the opposition increases so do the holes. The institution of the Lord's Supper at the time of the Passover is symbolically loaded, as is Jesus' insistence that his imminent crucifixion is not accidental but is "as it has been determined" (22:22). The Jewish opposition to Jesus, as depicted by Luke, though not uniform (24:50–56), is tragic. A "war of interpretation" is underway in which Jesus' identity is grasped by unlikely people but rejected by most of the Jewish religious leaders.

H. The Resurrection and Ascension (Luke 24:1–53)

Luke 24 paints vividly the story of the resurrection, Jesus' appearances to his disciples, his commissioning them as witnesses—a major theme in Acts—and his ascension. Gabriel had early on informed Mary that Jesus would occupy the throne of David, and at the outset of the Travel Narrative we are informed that Jesus will be "taken up." Here, in the climax of Luke's Gospel, these predictions are fulfilled in Jesus' enthronement as Lord over the universe. At the same time, Luke 24 and Acts 1 provide the transition from the story of Jesus to that of the witnesses.

It is indeed a powerful story. Joel B. Green captures the theme of Luke's narrative as follows:

> Throughout, the Lukan narrative focuses attention on a pervasive, coordinating theme: salvation. Salvation is neither ethereal nor merely future, but embraces life in the present, restoring the integrity of human life, revitalizing human communities, setting the cosmos in order, and commissioning the community of God's people to put God's grace into practice among themselves and toward ever-widening circles of others. The Third Evangelist knows nothing of such dichotomies as those sometimes drawn between social and spiritual or individual and communal. Salvation embraces the totality of embodied life, including its social, economic, and political concerns. For Luke, the God of Israel is the Great Benefactor whose redemptive purpose is manifest in the career of Jesus, whose message is that this benefaction enables and inspires new ways for living in the world.[20]

SUGGESTED READING

☐   If you have the time, read through the Gospel of Luke as a unit. If not, take one or two of the sections above and read carefully through them.

Reflection

Do you find it helpful to read Luke's Gospel as a true story about Jesus? Explain your answer.

_____

_____

_____

By yourself or in a group, try to paraphrase the high points of Luke's story of Jesus, moving through the major events he narrates. Use your Bible as you move along!

_____

_____

_____

_____

_____

Imagine yourself as a first-century Gentile listening to Luke's story of Jesus. What stands out for you?

_____

_____

_____

THE CENTRALITY OF PRAYER IN JESUS' LIFE AND MINISTRY

The vision evoked by Luke is enormous, difficult as it may be for those of us who have grown up initiated in this reality to comprehend or appreciate. Salvation is available to everyone, and the disciples are called to be at the heart of the *missio Dei*, the mission of God. But how are we to live and participate effectively in God's mission? A major answer provided by Luke is *through prayer*. Indeed, Luke has rightly been referred to as "the evangelist of prayer."[1] It is not by chance that this Gospel writer refers to Jesus praying at *seven* crucial points during his ministry (3:21; 5:16; 6:12; 9:18; 11:1; and 22:41). Only the last has parallels in the other Gospels (Matt 26:39; Mark 14:35). The number seven symbolizes completeness and fullness in Scripture,

> The number seven symbolizes completeness and fullness in Scripture, and Luke portrays Jesus as the exemplar of the prayerful human being.

and Luke portrays Jesus as the exemplar of the prayerful human being.

Luke's Gospel thus uniquely emphasizes prayer.
This is not to say that Luke presents a different Jesus
from the one portrayed in the other Gospels, but
rather that he deliberately opens the window for us
on the place of prayer in Jesus' life and public ministry. All three Synoptic Gospels (Matthew, Mark,
and Luke) note Jesus' pattern of withdrawing to pray
in the midst of his public ministry (5:16; Matt 14:23;
Mark 1:35), but time and again Luke positions prayer
in the foreground in a way the other Gospels do not.
Indeed, prayer is pervasive in Luke's Gospel.

Luke records that when Zechariah went into the
most holy place to burn incense, "all the assembled
worshipers were praying outside" (1:11, emphasis added). In the context of such prayer and worship in the
temple, an angel appears to Zechariah and instructs
him, "Do not be afraid, Zechariah; your prayer has
been heard. Your wife Elizabeth will bear you a son,
and you are to call him John" (1:13). Mary's Song (the
Magnificat) follows in 1:46–55. Hers is a great prayer
of praise, brimming with Old Testament vocabu-
lary, as Mary celebrates what the Lord is now doing.
Zechariah's song combines praise and prophecy as
he too borrows from the Old Testament to praise the
Lord for his fulfillment of long-cherished promises.

Simeon's prayer (2:29–32) will be familiar to many.
Luke depicts Simeon as a man of prayer; he was "righteous and devout," "waiting" (a critical characteristic
of prayer), and "the Holy Spirit was on him." God had
revealed to Simeon that he would not die before see-
ing the Messiah; indeed, the Spirit moves him to be

present in the temple at the precise moment Joseph and Mary present Jesus there, and Simeon takes Jesus into his arms and praises God. Luke reveals that Anna, the aged prophetess, "never left the temple but worshiped night and day, fasting and praying" (2:37). We might liken Anna to a contemplative nun. Approaching the holy family, she "gave thanks to God" before addressing the crowd about the child (2:36–38).

It is not by chance that these early recognitions of Jesus as the Messiah take place *in the temple*. The temple was the location where God lived amid his people, and as such it was the symbolic center of the Jewish universe. In these early chapters we see the temple functioning, according to its design, as the place of worship and prayer. The boy Jesus referred to the temple as "my Father's house" (2:49).

A distinctive feature of Luke's Gospel, as we have seen, is Jesus' long journey toward Jerusalem, the city of the temple. In Luke 19:41–42 we read that as Jesus approaches Jerusalem and sees the city, he weeps over it because on this auspicious day Jerusalem is unable to recognize the One who will bring it peace. That lack of recognition is immediately focused on the temple as Jesus drives out those who are hawking their wares within the courtyard of the sacred precinct. Luke 19:46 alludes to two Old Testament texts, Isaiah 66:7 and Jeremiah 7. Jesus' indictment against the religious leaders is that they have transformed the temple into something different from its intended identity, reducing it from a "house of prayer" to a "den of robbers" (19:45–46)—a reference to an extraordinarily powerful sermon that Jeremiah delivered outside the temple gates as Israelites were coming to worship (Jer 7:1–11). In Jeremiah 7:11 Yahweh asks, "Has this house, which bears my Name, become a den of robbers to you?" The "house of prayer" reference comes from Isaiah 66:7, which is part of a beautiful passage in which Yahweh declares his intention for Israel to be a missional people, with foreigners coming to worship in the temple: "For my house will be called a house of prayer for all nations."

The temple is a major metaphor for the Church in the New Testament (e.g., 1 Pet 2:4–10). Jesus' cleansing of the temple (19:45) is a prophetic sign that he is in the process of creating a new temple. As Peter puts it, we are living stones being built into a spiritual house (or temple) to be a holy priesthood, offering spiritual sacrifices to God through Jesus Christ. We are a chosen people, a royal priesthood, a holy nation, a people belonging to God, so that we may declare his praises; once we were not a people, but now we are the people of God. For us to be the temple is for us to participate in that communion, which is the very life of God! If that is true of us, then we too—filled as we are with God—can be referred to as houses of prayer.

Matthew and Mark write of Jesus' baptism by John, the opening of the heavens, the descent of the Spirit, and the voice from heaven. Luke includes all of this, adding a reference to Jesus' prayer (3:21–22). It was precisely as Jesus was praying that heaven opened, the Spirit descended as a dove, and the Father spoke from aloft. Prayer facilitates the open heaven of Jesus' baptism and is central to—the engine of—how God manages his world. In Luke, the story of Jesus' baptism immediately precedes his genealogy (3:21–22). At his baptism the Father declares Jesus to be "my Son, the Beloved," and in the genealogy that follows Jesus' ancestry is traced back to "Adam, son of God." Jesus' sonship is, of course, far more than human, but his divine Sonship manifests itself in his humanity as the second Adam. This raises the question of whether an exploration of divine Fatherhood and Sonship can lead us into a deeper understanding of God's plan and purpose, so that we too can live beneath an open heaven, have the Spirit descend upon us, and hear the Father pronounce us beloved. Luke's answer is clear: This can only be true as we are praying!

Matthew and Mark tell us that Jesus called and sent out 12 disciples, giving them authority to cast out evil spirits and to heal. The Twelve includes Judas Iscariot, "who became a traitor." But Luke's narrative includes two references to prayer on the occasion of Jesus' calling of the Twelve: "One of those days, Jesus went out to a mountainside to pray, and spent the night praying to God. When morning came he called his disciples and chose twelve of them, whom he also designated apostles" (6:12–13, 16). Luke thus alerts us that the choice of Judas, Jesus' betrayer, was no mistake, and neither was the choice of the remaining 11 who would constitute the foundation of the new people of God. Jesus' mission, including its continuation through the apostles, is from the outset grounded and enveloped in prayer.

> Jesus' mission, including its continuation through the apostles, is from the outset grounded and enveloped in prayer.

A similar distinction is found between Luke and Matthew and Mark in relation to Peter's confession

(9:18–20), the turning point in all three Synoptic Gospels. Only Luke mentions that Jesus had been "praying in private" just prior to asking the question about his identity that led to Peter's confession of Jesus as "God's Messiah" (9:20). In Luke 9 Jesus goes on to inform his disciples that he must suffer—a teaching followed by the narrative of his transfiguration (9:28–36). Jesus takes his disciples up onto the mountainside to pray, and it is as Jesus is praying that his true status is disclosed to Peter, James, and John: He is the one who fulfills the Law (Moses) and the Prophets (Elijah) as the Son of God. The account of Jesus' discussion with Moses and Elijah uses the evocative Greek word ἔξοδος (exodus) to describe Jesus' departure. Peter is so overwhelmed that he proposes setting up three dwellings—one each for Moses, Elijah, and Jesus—inadvertently signaling that he is missing the entire point of Jesus' mission. Jesus must descend from the mountain to fulfill his mission of leading the entire creation in an exodus from sin and judgment. He has gone up the mountain to pray, but Peter, James, and John nearly miss the transfiguration on account of their sleepiness (9:32). Emerging from his prayer, Jesus discusses his "exodus" with Moses and Elijah, but Peter's mistaken proposal is interrupted by the Father's voice bearing witness to Jesus as "my Son," to whom they should listen. Prayer here, as in many other places in Luke's Gospel, sets the context for and facilitates the disclosure of Jesus to his disciples.

Prayer is clearly a major emphasis in Luke's Gospel, absolutely central to Jesus' life and ministry. Whereas in Matthew 6 the Lord's Prayer is part of the Sermon on the Mount, in Luke 11 the different context is instructive. As Jews, the disciples would have been inducted into the act of praying from early childhood. But they notice something tangibly different about Jesus' prayer life (see 11:1). Observing Jesus pray, it occurs to them that they have no real idea how to pray, spurring their request, "Lord, teach us to pray, just as John taught his disciples." We have no idea how John went about teaching his disciples to pray, but Jesus teaches them the Lord's Prayer and then provides instruction about perseverance in prayer (9:2–13; see also 18:1–6; 20:47 on the hiddenness of prayer; 21:36 on prayer as vigilance; 22:32 on prayer failure; 22:40, 46 on prayer and temptation; and 22:41–44 on prayer and suffering).

At Jesus' baptism the Father proclaims, "You are my beloved Son; with you I am well pleased" (3:22). He again asserts at the transfiguration, "This is my Son," and at his death the Son cries out, "Father, into your hands I commit my spirit" (23:46). Between these central moments Jesus instructs his disciples to call upon his Father as their Father—even as he teaches them by word and example how costly it is to be his faithful child. Thus, as Tom Wright points out,

> The Lord's Prayer is not so much a command as an invitation: an invitation to share in the prayer-life of Jesus himself. Seen with Christian hindsight—more specifically, with Trinitarian perspective—the Lord's Prayer becomes an invitation to share in the divine life itself. It becomes one of the high roads into the central mystery of Christian salvation and Christian existence: that the

> baptized and believing Christian is (1) in-
> corporated into the inner life of the triune
> God and (2) intended not just to believe
> that this is the case, but actually to experi-
> ence it.[2]

In Luke, Jesus' teaching of the Lord's Prayer comes not long after his transfiguration and shortly after the mission of the 70. As Wright observes, "Its every clause resonates with Jesus' announcement that God's kingdom is breaking into the story of Israel and the world, opening up God's long-promised new world and summoning people to share it."[3] This commentator justifiably reads the Lord's Prayer against the background of Old Testament exodus motifs and points out that the prayer embodies Jesus' own mission and vocation; it thereby invites Jesus' disciples into a process of becoming, forming them into his co-workers in prayer for the kingdom. Jesus does not need to pray for forgiveness of sins, but this petition binds his disciples to his mission (see 24:47). Again, in Wright's words,

> The prayer is given by Jesus to constitute his
> followers as the true Exodus people. They
> are to succeed, not least by prayer, where
> the original wilderness generation failed.
> The prayer moves from the disciples' rela-
> tion to God, through the honoring of God's
> name and the doing of his will, to provi-
> sions for bodily needs and dealing with evil.
> Furthermore, the prayer has something
> of the same shape—and, within the new
> eschatological moment, something of the

same role—as the Decalogue within the Exodus narrative. Thus the Lord's Prayer may be seen as being to the church as the Ten Commandments were to Israel: not just something to do, a comparatively arbitrary rule of life, but the heart of the new covenant charter.[4]

Wright insightfully notes that the Lord's Prayer should shape our liturgical, corporate worship as well as our personal prayer. The role of the temple in Luke indicates that Jesus participated in prescribed, communal prayer and worship. However, the radical innovation and focus in this book is on Jesus' personal practice of prayer. Needless to say, the two ought to complement one another.

The story of Jesus' visit to Mary and Martha—material that is also unique to Luke—comes at the end of Luke 10 and immediately prior to the Lord's Prayer. In this story, Mary exemplifies the welcome of Jesus that is appropriate to discipleship. The fourfold repetition of "Lord" showcases Jesus' authority, and Mary's position at Jesus' feet signifies submission and attentiveness. As Green points out, "The welcome Jesus seeks is not epitomized in distracted, worrisome domestic performance, but in attending to this guest whose very presence is a disclosure of the divine plan."[5] The word "prayer" does not occur in this story, but there is a long tradition of associating Mary with (contemplative) prayer.[6] Thus, Merton comments:

Is there anything in the Gospels about the contemplative life? What is the value of the Mary-Martha story? It seems to me that the literal sense is plain, and that the superiority of contemplation over action is explicitly stated there. But as St. Thomas himself proves—and the whole life of Jesus shows—the supreme Christian life is one which shares the fruits of contemplation with others.[7]

There is a danger here of reading into the text, but if we think of prayer as that attitude whereby we "wish to hear his word and respond to it with our whole being,"[8] it is clearly appropriate to see in this account instruction about prayer. Augustine discerns the richness of the story when he asks, "What was Mary enjoying? What was she eating? I'm persistent on this point, because I'm enjoying it too. I will venture to say that she was eating the one she was listening to."[9] The context confirms this impression: Mary's attentiveness to Jesus is mirrored shortly afterward by Jesus' attentiveness to the Father in prayer.

The prayer parables unique to Luke are those of the shameless beggar-neighbor (11:5–8); the marginalized, seemingly helpless widow, who persistently pursues and at last receives justice from the wicked judge, who is not at all like the God climactically revealed in Jesus (18:1–8); and the self-assured Pharisee and the appropriately humbled tax-collector (18:9–14). In 11:5–13, immediately following the Lord's Prayer, the theme of bread as representative of hospitality, perseverance, and the wonderful goodness of the Father takes center stage.

Matthew, Mark, and Luke all tell of Jesus' struggle in prayer in the garden of Gethsemane. The same three Gospel writers all report Jesus' prediction, just prior to that incident, of Peter's betrayal, yet only Luke records Jesus' words of assurance to Peter: "But I have prayed for you, that your faith may not fail. And when you have turned again, strengthen your brothers" (22:32). Prayer functions here, as Søren Kierkegaard notes, as a sign of Jesus' great love. Jesus is not asking Peter to change; he loves this disciple just as he is, and that love will help Peter become a better man.[10]

Finally, Matthew and Mark record Jesus' cry of dereliction on the cross: his quotation of the first line of Psa 22, a psalm of great hope in the midst of suffering. Matthew and Mark tell us that Jesus cried out at his death, but only Luke adds that these last words were a prayer: "Father, into your hands I commit my spirit!" (23:46, a quote from Psa 31:5–6).[11] And Luke alone records the earlier, remarkable intercession, "Father, forgive them, for they know not what they do" (23:34). The one who taught his disciples to pray by word and by example, even for their enemies—again according to Luke alone—did precisely that from the cross for those very ones who had crucified him.

Finally, Luke's Gospel ends with prayer; we find ourselves transported into the company of a band of overjoyed disciples returning to Jerusalem, there to bless God continually in the same temple in which Zechariah had fallen mute. But first they are blessed by the risen Christ (24:50–53). For Luke, the gospel is about God being present among his people, and about his people being attentive to his presence. As Jean Vanier notes of John 1, "At one moment in time the 'Logos' became flesh and entered history. He came to lead us all into this communion which is the very life of God."[12] Jesus' life is centered in deep relationship with the Father, and everything in his ministry is an extension of this relationship; indeed, the goal of his ministry is to lead us into communion with God.

SUGGESTED READING

☐   Read through each section referred to above in which Luke emphasizes Jesus' prayer life.

Reflection

Reflect on how Luke begins and ends his Gospel. What is the role of prayer in these Gospel bookends? How does this role differ from the beginning to the end?

_____

_____

_____

_____

Consider one of the events discussed above. Why does Luke alert us to Jesus' praying in relation to this event? What can we as disciples learn from this?

_____

_____

_____

_____

PRAYER AND THE STORY OF REDEMPTION IN LUKE

We have read the story of Jesus from Luke's perspective. We have zoomed in on the many references to prayer in Luke's Gospel. Now we need to explore the connections between the two. To excavate Luke's theology of prayer, we need to read his discussions of prayer in the context of the grand story he narrates.

DIVINE ECONOMY

Theologians often refer to the grand story of which Jesus is the climax as the "divine economy." The "economy" refers to God's plan for this world and how he manages the world toward his goal for it.[1] Our focus on the coupling of Jesus and prayer in Luke alerts us that this divine economy is relational through and through; it is inherently Trinitarian. If we are ever in danger of thinking about God's sovereignty and providence mechanically, Luke prompts us to resist such a view.

Prayer is a profound expression of relationship with God and, in Jesus' case, of the interpersonal nature of the biblical God. Mysteriously, God is interpersonal *within himself*, and the drama of Scripture is enacted in its climax in Luke through the deep interconnections among Jesus, the Father, and the Spirit. We discover Jesus in prayer, in deep communion with the Father by the Spirit, at every crucial step in his public ministry. The path for the great drama to proceed to its climax is laid by prayer. Jesus prays at his baptism, the heavens open, and the Father affirms the Son's coming journey to the cross for sinners. Jesus spends a night in prayer before choosing 12 disciples, 11 of whom will form the basis for the new people of God who will emerge in Luke's sequel, the Acts of the Apostles. Jesus goes up onto a mountain to pray, leading to his transfiguration, during which Moses and Elijah discuss with him his coming "departure"; the Greek word used in this passage may be rendered "exodus," reminding us that Jesus' death is aimed at nothing less than leading the whole creation out of its slavery in the direction of freedom. As he heads into his passion week, Jesus prays and is strengthened by an angel from heaven (22:43). Even on the cross, as we have seen, Jesus prays.

> A significant insight of Luke's Gospel is that prayer facilitates the disclosure of Jesus—first Jesus' own prayer, and second the prayers of his people.

The climax (warp) of the great drama of redemption is thus woven throughout the fabric of the narrative through the weft of prayer, intertwined with the deep relationship among Father, Son, and Spirit.

The divine economy is also that into which people are invited to participate; a significant insight of Luke's Gospel is that prayer facilitates the disclosure of Jesus—first Jesus' own prayer, and second the prayers of his people. As D. M. Crump notes,

> Luke associates the prayers of Jesus with the acquisition of spiritual insight at key locations throughout his gospel. ... Luke presents Jesus primarily, though not exclusively, as an Intercessor whose prayers on behalf of the disciples serve to accomplish all that is required for successful, obedient discipleship— including their calling, illumination and perseverance. ... [I]t is in fact the prayers of Jesus which mediate ... spiritual perception.[2]

Jesus' exultation concerning that which remains hidden from "the wise and understanding" but has been revealed to "little children" (10:21–22) constitutes a prayer of thanksgiving, which similarly relates the disclosure of Jesus to the revealing work of the Father through the Son.[3]

As we have seen, the narrative of Luke's Gospel is bookended by prayer—a literary device called an inclusio. The story begins with Zechariah in the temple. While the community prays outdoors, an angel appears within to announce Yahweh's answer to the priest's particular prayer concerning his barren wife. The story of righteous Zechariah and Elizabeth has become the latest critical moment in this redemptive narrative replete with persons summoned to believe God's promises and play their respective parts in God's great drama. But this particular "righteous" one—who is presented here as something of a failure—reminds us of so many others within the biblical and historical narrative thus far. Luke's Gospel opens with a priest who is providentially brought into the temple and later returns to God's expectant people unable to speak, and thus unable to bless them—for unbelief has rendered him mute. Silence is imposed upon Zechariah—a silence during the course of which he can contemplate Gabriel's message and prepare himself, in obedience, to name his son John.

Luke's Gospel also closes with prayer, with a band of elated disciples returning to Jerusalem and then blessing God continually in the same temple in which Zechariah had fallen mute. But first these disciples are blessed by the risen and ascending Christ (24:50-53). The One who voluntarily identified with the sinfulness of God's covenant people when he submitted to baptism by the son of the once muted priest—the same One who claimed to be playing the part of Israel's Messiah, who was rejected as such by the temple authorities and the throngs gathered in the royal city, who prayed for his enemies when they crucified him, and who prayed to his Father as he died at the ninth hour (the same hour during which Zechariah would have been in the temple to offer incense)[4]—*has arisen* (24:1-8). The first installment of Luke's twofold

> The first installment of Luke's twofold story ends with the risen One blessing his people as he ascends into heaven, receiving worship from a new community of blessed ones who in turn are blessing God (24:50-53).

story ends with the risen One blessing his people[5] as he ascends into heaven, receiving worship from a new community of blessed ones who in turn are blessing God (24:50–53).[6]

Different characters in this drama respond differently to its climax in Jesus. One man at the beginning of Luke's work, Zechariah, cannot believe Gabriel's auspicious words. But a young girl, Mary, does believe when the same angel visits her. Similarly, when Jesus is resurrected at the end of the first volume, the news comes first to a band of women (including two women named Mary) from two angelic spokespersons. When the women conveyed these joyous words to the gathered disciples, their report "seemed like an idle tale, and they," like Zechariah, "did not believe" (24:11).[7]

Luke's narrative is indeed full of people who should be prepared to understand what God is doing in and through Jesus but either cannot or will not.[8] Still, some characters are prepared and participate with joy over what they see and hear.[9] How are the prayers of Anna (in light of her own perception) and of Jesus (in light of his disciples' evolving perception—both before Peter's confession at the transfiguration and at the table with the disciples in Emmaus) related to this aspect of Luke's story? Quite integrally: We see this from the confession of Peter at the transfiguration, when he recognizes and acknowledges Jesus' true identity, and from that of Cleopas and his companion, both of which are tied to Jesus' prayer (24:30–31). Tom Wright has pointed out that there is a remarkable inclusio between Genesis 3:7—"Then the eyes of both were opened"—and Luke 24:31—"their eyes were opened." This inclusio alerts us to the comprehensive scope of Christ's redemptive work: a setting right of that which had gone wrong in God's good creation. For our purposes it is instructive to note that Jesus' prayer facilitates the overcoming of the first, fatal opening of eyes through the second, redemptive opening of eyes.

It is clear that we have in Luke's Gospel more than isolated, unrelated instances of prayer. Luke associates prayer with the forward thrust of God's redemptive drama, with gaining or disclosing insight into the reality of that drama and its central character, and with preparation for participation in its unfolding. Thus, as D. M. Crump observes, considering "the way in which prayer serves to attune the will of the individual to the will of God ... Luke reveals various ways in which God is already guiding salvation-history, and prayer is a means of human perception of, and thus participation in, what God is doing."[10] God, we might say, manages his economy through relationships, and prayer is the deepest expression of this interconnectedness.

Throughout Luke's Gospel, prayer is indispensable to the manner in which characters within the story align themselves—not only with the way in which God's continuing story is reaching its climax but also with how this climax challenges shallow perspectives concerning God's identity and nature. Those who hear this story are faced with a call concerning their present lives and God's purposes, as narrated by Luke. Luke introduces us to characters who critically judge the drama unfolding in Jesus based upon prior commitments and privileges they are unwilling to relinquish. These individuals fail to enter God's redemptive activity in the world and are thus doomed, having forsaken the key to knowledge (11:37–52). But those who pray with Jesus learn to call upon the God of Israel as "Father"; to relate to him as kind, caring, and benevolent; and to repent of selfish, fearful, violent, slavish, destructive, and dehumanizing orientations, in order further to align themselves with him and his purposes, clarified by Jesus' portrayal of and teaching about his Father and his own messianic vocation (4:16–44; 5:27–32; 7:18–35; 8:1, 4–15; 9:1–6, 18–22, 37–44; 10:21–24; 11:2–4; see also 6:20–38; 12:22–34; 14:15–24; 15:1–32; 18:1–8, 15–34; 19:1–10; 20:9–18, 41–44; 22:7–22, 28–30, 35–38; 23:39–43; 24:25–27, 30–32, 36–49).

SUGGESTED READING
☐   Luke 9:18–36

Reflection

The turning point in Matthew, Mark, and Luke is Peter's confession that Jesus is the Messiah.

How does Luke's portrayal of Jesus praying in Luke 9:18 affect the way we read the story of Peter's remarkable confession?

_____

_____

_____

What does "Messiah" mean, and why would prayer have been vital to Peter's arriving at this insight?

_____

_____

_____

What is disclosed about Jesus in the transfiguration (9:28–36)?

_____

_____

_____

THE ACTS OF THE APOSTLES—PART 2

Although our focus in this commentary is on Luke, it is worth noting briefly how the emphasis on prayer continues in Acts. The first volume of Luke's story ends with the risen Messiah blessing his people as he ascends into heaven, receiving worship from a new community of blessed ones who in turn bless God. But in God's economy, being blessed by God and blessing him in return involves being a blessing to others.[1] In his second volume, Luke narrates the initial extension of this blessing to all nations.

> In God's economy, being blessed by God and blessing him in turn involves being a blessing to others.

Luke's story begins in Jerusalem, but, taking the second volume into account, ends in Rome. Acts comes to its end with Paul imprisoned in Rome "proclaiming the kingdom of God and teaching about the Lord Jesus Christ with all boldness and without hindrance" (Acts 28:31). The story is thus one of movement and fulfillment, for God himself is on the move (keeping promises, answering prayer, filling a people, working miracles, stretching out his hand, setting prisoners free, spreading his people abroad, and overseeing their participation in his redemptive mission). God is doing something new in the world, first through his Spirit-empowered Servant, Jesus (3:22; 4:1, 14, 18–19), and then (and now) through the Spirit-filled followers of Jesus (11:11–13; 24:48–49; Acts 1:4–8; 2:1–21). But this new thing is none other than that which had been promised from of old, the same thing for which faithful Israel had for so long been waiting. The story of national Israel has reached its divinely intended climax—it is time for Yahweh's renewed temple-people to become a house of prayer made up of all nations.

Just as Jesus is continuously portrayed in the first volume as being on a mission for God and tuned in to God's plan through prayer, so in his sequel Luke portrays his disciples as being in continuity with him, as Joel Green notes, "particularly with regard to the practice of prayer."[2] Thus, "in Acts, prayer is (1) a means by which God's aim is disclosed and discerned, and (2) the means by which people get in sync with and participate in what God is doing."[3] Green cites other, evidently deliberate parallels between Luke's two volumes, such as those of Jesus and the disciples praying before their reception of the Spirit for ministry (3:21; Acts 1:14; 2:1–4; 8:15–17), Jesus and his disciples praying before they select apostles (6:12; Acts 1:24), and Jesus and Stephen praying as they face death for the forgiveness of their persecutors (23:34; Acts 7:60). Citing much more evidence, including more than 30 references to prayer throughout Acts, as well as the presence of prayer within significant narrative summaries, Green hones in on the central point that "Luke establishes Jesus' followers as persons who continue to model the piety of Jesus. ... [T]he devotion of these disciples speaks volumes about their fundamental orientation to the purpose of God, their alignment with the will of God, and their conviction that God will hear and respond to their prayers."[4]

The kingdom activity of prayer is a fitting way for disciples to participate in God's kingdom power because, while prayer constitutes a dual confession of our weakness, on the one hand, and of God's power, on the other (Acts 4:24–28), genuine acts of prayer assume that this powerful God has invited our participation (Acts 4:29–31; see also Acts 40:36–37).[5] To pray as one summoned into kingdom service is to take on a serious and strategic role in preparation for participating further as a disciple of the King, as he works his holy but often mysterious will.[6]

Thus, while prayer is not a brand of technology intended to induce or even coerce God to act, it is a reminder that God invites our participation in his redemptive plans. As Green points out, "Throughout Acts, prayer provides an opportunity for the disclosure of God's purpose."[7] Christians pray to gain a grasp of God's purposes (or to be grasped by them); to take up our part in doing God's will; and to express our faith, hope, and longing to see God's will done in the world. In Luke's two volumes, aligning oneself with God's purposes clarifies not only God's will for the moment but also the meaning of the Scriptures. To this end, prayer in these two volumes is a practice presented to us that we might embrace, discern, persevere in, and be transformed by the good news of God's kingdom.[8] In Luke's second volume particularly, as Green reminds us, "prayer is put forward as one of the ways in which God's will becomes manifest, both in the sense that in prayer the divine will is disclosed and in the sense that in prayer humans align themselves with God's will."[9]

> Christians pray to gain a grasp of God's purposes (or to be grasped by them); to take up our part in doing God's will; and to express our faith, hope, and longing to see it done in the world.

SUGGESTED READING

☐   Acts 4:23–31

Reflection

Make a list of the elements of the believer's prayer in Acts 4:24-28.

_____

_____

_____

_____

What can we learn from this about prayer?

_____

_____

_____

_____

What did these disciples request in their prayer? How does this relate back to Luke's Gospel?

_____

_____

_____

_____

PRAYER AND READING LUKE

In Luke, the kingdom comes through prayer, through the intimate communion between Father, Son, and Spirit. Through prayer—Jesus' own and that of believers—Jesus' true identity as the king is disclosed, and we are able to see him for who he is and to follow him fruitfully.

There is much to learn from this, as we will see in greater detail below. For now, it should be noted that apart from prayer we will never properly understand either the Gospel of Luke or the Bible as a whole. Luke's story concentrates on the climax in the economy of God in the great drama of salvation. As we have seen, God's economy is inherently relational; it is Trinitarian and, most remarkably, a story designed to invite us to share in God's life and mission. The Bible, and Luke in particular, do not just relate the true story of the world but invite us to become participants in that story. Prayer as communion with God is a God-given, and therefore indispensable, means that enables us to grasp and live within this drama. If the story is true, how could we possibly grasp it if it does not grasp us and draw us to "enter the kingdom" by bowing before the King?

Prayer is essential to the interpretation of Scripture because acceptable prayer is the opposite of self-sufficiency (Luke 18)—and since the Scriptures are revelation, no one has access to them apart from God's gracious gift (2:25–32, 36–38; 10:21–22; 16:19–31; 24:13–49; Acts 10; 13:44–49; 16:14). Luke narrates the prayers of Jesus and his early followers because he believes that similar practices will have similar desirable effects upon those who hear and respond in faith to his narrative presentation of Jesus.

Sadly, books on biblical interpretation rarely deal with prayer or even list the topic in their indices, and searches of journal databases reveal very few articles that address it. A major characteristic of modernity has been the privatization of religion, whereby the "scientific" nature of academic work is protected from religion, which is thought to contaminate academic work and public life and is thus confined to the private dimensions of our lives. In biblical studies, the result has often been an iron wall, with biblical interpretation on the one side and faith and church life on the other. Christian faith resists such privatization and compartmentalization. Academic study of the Bible is useful and vital, especially if practiced as an outgrowth of faith.

One thing we can learn from the manner in which Luke narrates his two-volume story of Jesus and his people fulfilling God's redemptive mission is that we need to recommit ourselves to reading and studying Scripture—with prayerfulness both literally and metaphorically at its center and with the understanding that research, teaching, and reading are (self-consciously Spirit-dependent) tasks on the way to faithful kingdom reception, participation, and performance. This approach in no way implies an abandonment of the tools and benefits of biblical study. It merely seeks to place those endeavors in a wider context—to see scholarly methods as tools meant to open texts for communities of faith in light of the Church's vocation to receive, celebrate, and display the realities to which the Scriptures bear witness. Our Lord has conferred upon the Church the task of presenting to the world this Act of God's drama.

Scholarly work on the Bible is crucial, but to exalt learning above humble prayer in the interest of understanding is to play the part of the self-sufficient Pharisee in Luke 18. Having accomplished all the work required of us, we should rather remember that we are mere servants and, beating our chests like the toll-collector, continue asking for interpretive wisdom. This theme is central to Jean-Louis Chrétien's rich work *Under the Gaze of the Bible*. This author rightly observes that

> the sage, for Christianity, is not the master of truth (for God alone is that) but the witness of truth, the one who attests—body and soul, and perhaps limping like Jacob after his struggle with the angel—that he has encountered a truth that is not himself but that has called him forever, knowing that the holy name of Christ, which he hopes to have on the tip of his tongue till his last

breath, opens his lips only to drink at the eternal source.[1]

For this reason, prayer, as a fitting activity through which to participate in the drama rendered in Scripture, should be woven into the fabric of Bible reading and interpretation. *Prayer is a necessary means of opening oneself to God and aligning oneself with his redemptive mission,* apart from which meaningful interpretation of the Bible *as Scripture* is impossible.[2] John Paul II asserts that "to arrive at a completely valid interpretation of words inspired by the Holy Spirit, one must first be guided by the Holy Spirit and it is necessary to pray for that, to pray much, to ask in prayer for the interior light of the Spirit and docilely accept that light, to ask for the love that alone enables one to understand the language of God, who 'is love' (1 John 1:8, 16)."[3]

Clifton Black offers a thorough exploration of this topic in an excellent article titled "Exegesis as Prayer" ("exegesis" is the technical word for interpreting the Bible). Black's work connects with John Paul's point about inspiration. Reflecting on Otto Piper's work on prayer in the Bible, Black points to Piper's insight that "prayer was not a religious auxiliary, a pietistic nod before getting down to the serious business of biblical exegesis. ... When proceeding in alignment with the same Spirit that animated scripture's creation and canonization within the church, *exegesis is an expression of prayer.*"[4]

In this light, Black suggests three prayerful dispositions that are indispensable for the exegete today—namely a capacity for holiness, a transfigured affection, and a disposition for thankful praise.[5] This type of exegesis requires overlapping communities of prayer and of interpretation:

> The practices of these two communities, however, do not always overlap. In our time, sad to say, much training in biblical scholarship occurs in settings where prayer has been severed from its task and responsibility, where the nurture of a faithful church is a *non sequitur*. Visits to the religious aisles of Barnes & Noble have become for me chilling summonses before the bar of judgment: much of what I find among the biblical resources are speculative fantasies, whether by Tim LaHaye or the Jesus Seminar. To my shame there is comparatively little that invites the church's laity or even curious passersby into the mysterious world of biblical faith that questions us, little to remind a reader that exegesis, like prayer, is not a cold conjecture but relationship with God so madly in love with us and the world that only the foolishness of the cross makes sense (1 Cor 1:18–31). Cruciform exegesis resembles petitionary prayer in this respect: if serious, its practitioner is inextricably bound up with its fulfillment (Matt 25:31–46).[6]

Joel Green is correct in stating that "Luke's Model Readers will embrace this narrative as their own, and seek to continue it in their lives ... ," taking up our roles "by embracing, indwelling, and embodying the divine story."[7] One of Luke's primary ways of signifying this is by depicting Jesus, those waiting for his first arrival, and those living in the wake of his "exodus" as people dedicated to prayer (Acts 1:14; 2:42). They are people who relate to God as a kind and merciful Father and thereby openly accept his narration of themselves into the same drama, as his children (18:15–17), with a growing awareness of the significance of the times (12:54–56; Acts 2:14–40; 3:24; 13:16–41; see also 1 Cor 10:1–11; Heb 1:1–2:4; 1 Pet 1:10–12, 17–21).

PRAYER IS ...

Prayer, taking the form both of quiet contemplation and of active participation, is an indispensable condition for the disclosure of Jesus, and so it must be for an exegesis that seeks to find the imagination of the exegete transformed by the drama announced and interpreted in and by Scripture. Prayer is the sense of being present to the Father in dependence, and thankfulness is utterly basic to responding to the invitation to participate in the great drama of the Bible; it must also be basic for understanding that drama and living it out today.

Thus, our prayer is more fully eschatological— end-times oriented—than Simeon's or Anna's. They prayed for the consolation of Israel—that God would maintain covenant faithfulness. Knowing Jesus, we experience the covenant faithfulness of God, and our prayers look backward for this fulfillment even as they look ahead to the final consummation (see 18:1–8 and 21:34–36 in light of 22:14–23; see also Acts 3:17–21 with 3:24).[8] Moreover, our prayer is characterized by a freedom and boldness of access into God's presence that is typified by the tabernacle and temple(s), and now realized through the self-offering of Jesus—an infinitely more competent priest than Zechariah. The book of Luke ends—and Acts begins—with the ascended Jesus blessing and directing his people. Luke's second volume interprets these blessings and this guidance as eschatological—that is, the risen Jesus blesses and guides through the ministry of the promised Spirit of restoration.[9] But already in the first volume the Spirit is a "gift" available to people who know God as an incomparably better Father than deficient earthly fathers (11:11-13). As J. Koenig explains,

> According to the apostolic witnesses, Jesus is our way to communicate with God at the turn of the ages (1 Cor. 1:4-9). When we acclaim him Kyrios [Lord] or address him as such, we are already speaking from an experience of the power, presence, and praise of God. But we are also asking, in his name, to enter more deeply into God's new creation, to take our own unique part, through prayer and action, in the final act of the divine drama.[10]

Jesus the Messiah, in whom we are blessed and through whom the age of the Israel-specific temple is brought to a close, invites us to share in his prayer life, to "know" the goodness of God,[11] and to relate to him in the way he did—as our Father. He who knows the Father uniquely (10:21-22) invites us to call upon his Father as our own (11:2b). Thus, the model prayer

given by Jesus is a prayer befitting those who come
to God in the stance of little children (10:21; 18:15–17).
The true Son (3:22, 38; 4:3, 9; 9:35; 10:21–22; 23:46), who
magnifies his Father's name (10:21), invites us to ori-
ent our lives for the same purpose: "Father, may your
name be regarded as sacred." We are to identify God
as Father and to consecrate ourselves as his true children by setting apart his name for honor.[12]

The Inaugurator of the kingdom—in that he is the
eschatological Son of David, Israel's true king who
must reign over the nations until all his enemies have
been subdued—teaches us to pray for its consummation (11:2).[13] We must learn to see ourselves as children
who long to see our Father's authority spread rather
than recede.

The One who taught concerning the reliability
and unfathomable beneficence of the Father and of
our great worth in his estimation (11:11–13; 12:22–32)
also teaches us to ask his and our Father for our daily
bread (11:3). Only those who know him as a kind and
merciful Father will be able to live as Jesus' brothers
and sisters and the Father's true children (6:27–36;
8:21; 9:46–48; 12:22–32; 23:34, 46).

He who calls tax collectors to be close associates
(6:27–28), deigns to dine with sinners (6:29–32; 7:31–35;
15:1–2; 19:1–10), and comes "to call sinners to repentance" (6:32) and "to seek and to save what was lost"
(19:10), describes himself as one "numbered with the
transgressors" (22:37). Moreover, this One, crucified
between two criminals even as he intercedes for the
forgiveness of his enemies, teaches us to ask the same
for ourselves and to release others from any indebted-
ness (11:4). The One who teaches us to ask the Father

for forgiveness is the same One who established the new covenant with his blood, even as he shared the table with his betrayer (22:20-21). He is the same One who announced Simon's future failure *and recovery* through a reference to his intercession (22:31-32). Indeed, the One who teaches us to ask our Father for forgiveness is the Father's true Son, in whose name "repentance and forgiveness of sins" are to be proclaimed to all nations (24:47; see also Acts 2:38; 5:31).

This One who sent out his disciples as lambs before wolves (10:3) teaches us to turn to our Father in anticipation of potential "temptation" (11:4), whether composed of trials that invite us to faithlessness, enticements to turn away more generally, or unbelief that might put God to the test. In any case the remedy is the same: Jesus teaches his disciples to depend upon God, our Father.[14] "The Lord's prayer," as N. T. Wright reminds us, "is an invitation to share Jesus' own prayer life—and with it his agenda, his work, his pattern of life, his spirituality."[15] Jesus is inviting us to identify the God of Israel, freshly revealed in and by himself, as our Father and to identify ourselves as his children.

> Jesus is inviting us to identify the God of Israel, freshly revealed in and by himself, as our Father and to identify ourselves as his children.

According to the author of these two volumes, Jesus is Israel's long-awaited Messiah who ushers in a new day, a day of prayer for a new community that gathers in his name, calls upon God as Father, and is filled with the Gift he said His Father would give to those who ask (11:11-13)[16]—the very gift that enables us to hear God's address in Scripture.

> **SUGGESTED READING**
>
> ☐   Luke 18:9–14

Reflection

What does Luke 18:9–14 teach us about prayer?

_____

_____

_____

The Pharisee would have been a "biblical scholar." What do we learn from this about the role of biblical scholarship in helping us understand the Bible?

_____

_____

_____

How should prayer and faith-full reading of the Bible relate to biblical study?

_____

_____

_____

PRAYER AND FULL-TIME MINISTRY

According to Romans 12:1-2, we as believers are full-time servants of God. Indeed, offering ourselves as living sacrifices is our only appropriate response "in view of God's mercies" in Christ (Rom 12:1; see also Rom 1-11). The word "ministry" signifies service; thus, it is a caricature of the kingdom of God to suggest that only pastoral ministers or missionaries are in the full-time service of God. In recent years, few authors have written as authoritatively on prayer as has Eugene Peterson. In particular, this author addresses prayer in conjunction with the pastoral ministry, but we can learn much from his writing about prayer in all avenues of full-time Christian ministry—as in the ordinary Christian life.

In *Working the Angles*, Peterson suggests that the *external acts* of the pastorate—preaching, teaching, and administration—symbolized by the three sides of a triangle, are funded by and dependent upon three practices symbolized by the angles of the triangle. Hence the title of his book, *Working the Angles*. Focusing on the external acts of the pastorate can be a continual temptation, as its integrity and well-being depend upon the repetitive, ongoing practice of working the angles.

For Peterson, the three angles are prayer, reading Scripture, and providing spiritual direction.

Preaching

Prayer

Trigonometry
of the
Pastorate

Scripture

Spiritual
Direction

Teaching   Administration

These "three pastoral acts are so basic, so critical, that they determine the shape of everything else."[1] However, they are not openly observable; rather, they are quiet, private acts characterized by attending to God:

> None of these acts is public, which means that no one knows for sure whether or not we are doing any of them. People hear us pray in worship, they listen to us preach and teach from the Scriptures, they notice when we are listening to them in a conversation, but they can never know if we are attending to *God* in any of this. It doesn't

take many years in this business to realize
that we can conduct a fairly respectable
pastoral ministry without giving much
more than ceremonial attention to God. ...
Pastoral work disconnected from the angle
actions—the acts of attention to God in relation to myself, the biblical communities of
Israel and church, the other person—is no
longer given its shape by God. Working the
angles is what gives shape and integrity to
the daily work of pastors and priests. ... [I]f
we are careless with or dismiss the angles,
no matter how long or straight we draw the
lines we will not have a triangle, a pastoral ministry.[2]

In our consumer-driven, extroverted culture,
there is great temptation to focus on the externals
while ignoring this principle of working the angles.
These angles are closely intertwined, and we need to
explore each one, along with its symbiotic relationship to the others. In the present study we focus on
the angle of prayer. In my experience of the pastorate, prayer is certainly esteemed to be fundamental;
however, there is hardly any pressure from anyone to
practice it. We must be able to pray well in public and
are expected to speak knowledgably about prayer, but
I cannot recall anyone in leadership taking an interest in helping me develop a deep, rich prayer life that
would fund my ministry in the present and for years
to come. To the contrary, attention always seemed
to be focused on the external acts of ministry and
church growth.

I doubt my experience is uncommon. Indeed, the statistics with regard to prayer and pastors are discouraging, if not dismal. I understand that it is unusual for pastors to consistently spend even 20 minutes a day in prayer. Henri Nouwen agrees, noting that though few pastors will deny the importance of prayer, or even that prayer constitutes the most important dimension of their lives, too many spend little to no time in prayer. "They realize that they should not forget to pray, that they should take time to pray, and that prayer should be a priority in their lives. But all these 'shoulds' do not have the power to carry them over the enormous obstacle of their activism."[3]

My intention is not to criticize or bash ministers. I know well both the glory and the struggle of the pastoral ministry. I often tell people that the pastoral ministry is vastly different from the inside than the outside, involving as it does constant public ministry, along with the scrutiny and critique that accompany it. Ministers are always trying to be there for others, while still having to look after themselves and their families; they become immersed in other people's pain and often have little support in their own. No, I have no desire to hammer away at fellow pastors. Rather, my hope is that a fresh look at the role of prayer in Jesus' ministry, as portrayed in the Gospel of Luke, might reorient pastors in this respect in relation to our lives and ministries, and prove deeply refreshing in the process. Prayer is about attending to God in Christ, and

> Prayer is about attending to God in Christ, and ultimately there is nothing as good or as renewing as being found again and again by Christ.

ultimately there is nothing as good or as renewing as being found again and again by Christ.

The pastoral ministry is unique and indispensable, but it is only one among many diverse forms of full-time service to which God's people are called. Peterson notes that a person's spirituality will take a form appropriate to that individual's vocation. The triangle for a stay-at-home mom with young children, for instance, will look very different from that of a pastor. And the triangles of a teacher, artist, academic, marketer, mechanic, or unemployed person will again have their own distinctive features. However, all of the triangles have in common that hidden angle of prayer, as well as that angle of Scripture. In Scripture God addresses us, and in prayer we respond to God. Throughout its history, the Church has learned—often at great cost—that it is fatal to separate prayer from Scripture, or Scripture from prayer. Indeed, in Scripture God not only addresses us but, as the Psalms and the Lord's Prayer in particular reflect, teaches us how to respond in prayer.

SUGGESTED READING

☐ Luke 5:15–16

Reflection

How would you describe your full-time ministry?

_____

_____

_____

What role do prayer and Scripture play in your ministry?

_____

_____

_____

Try to map out your own "triangle of ministry" with its external acts and internal angles. Then ask yourself, "Am I working the angles?"

_____

_____

_____

WHY PRAYER MUST BE CENTRAL

Prayer must be central in all our lives because God must be central, and it is through prayer that we attend to God and open ourselves to him at the deepest level of our being. Jesus' judgment on and cleansing of the temple remind us powerfully of how easy it is to neglect prayer, and thus God. As we have noted, in the Old Testament the temple bears the name of the Lord. This means not only that the temple is symbolic of God's presence in heaven but that the Lord is truly present among his people, and the temple is the place where God's people meet with him. Thus, it is not surprising that in Isaiah God refers to the temple as "my house of prayer" (Isa 56:7), and Isaiah looks forward to the day when it will be such for all nations. The temple is about God in intimate, incarnate relationship to his people. It is the place of "my presence" (Jer 7:15), and prayer is about being attentive to God; thus, God's house is inevitably a house of prayer.

Jesus' description of the temple as having become a den of robbers comes from that amazing passage in Jer 7 in which the unenviable Jeremiah has to stand at the gate of the temple and proclaim a powerful message about deceptive words and worship: "Has this house, which bears my name, become a den of robbers to you?" asks the Lord (Jer 7:11).

Jesus cleanses the temple in Luke 19:45 because the house of prayer has been reduced to a mall—a shopping precinct. In 1 Peter 2:4–10 Peter tells us that we are being built into the new temple, a spiritual house offering spiritual sacrifices. This description of the Church reminds us that prayer should be at its heart. The temptation is always to make it something else: a business, a marketplace, a guarantee of safety—a den of robbers. This is a particularly real temptation in our postmodern culture, characterized as it is by consumerism. Alan Storkey notes just how powerfully our culture has capitulated to this emphasis: "Consumption is collectivist-individualist, nationalist-internationalist, the healer, the entertainer, the lover, the spiritual, the feeder and the consolation. It is the chief rival to God in our culture."[1] Storkey comments further, "Postmodernism is consumption. The deconstruction and fragmentation which [are] often identified with changes in approaches to text and philosophy [are] actually buying, advertisements, TV culture, in-your-face entertainment, shopping, pressure, thing-filled living—in a word consumption."[2]

The Church, to employ English understatement, has not been exempt from the seduction of consumerism. As David F. Wells notes,

> The cultural context in which we live favors
> those forms of spirituality, Christian and
> otherwise, that are marching to the tune
> of [modern] culture, rather than those that

are seeking to be faithful to the God of biblical revelation. What so many of these new spiritualities have in common is that they are offering benefits for the self and asking for little or no spiritual accountability. Designer religion of [our day] allows itself to be tailored to each personality. It gives but never takes; it satisfies inner needs but never asks for repentance; it offers mystery and asks for no service. It provides a sense of Something Other in life but never requires that we stand before that Other.[3]

And Eugene Peterson contextualizes this trend in terms of American pastors, lamenting,

The pastors of America have metamorphosed into a company of shopkeepers, and the shops they keep are churches. They are preoccupied with shopkeeper's concerns—how to keep the customers happy, how to lure customers away from competitors down the street, how to package the goods so that the customers will lay out more money.[4]

In this context, Luke's Gospel is a helpful corrective, reminding us that a gospel ministry is about the temple, and thus about prayer. Our practice of prayer, or the lack thereof, will embody our theology of church; it is so easy for the focus to slip so that relationship with God is made subservient to other goals. Jean Danielou rightly asserts that "the Churches justify their existence when they fulfill their function. If it is the function of the Churches to make prayer possible, the Churches justify themselves when through their efforts prayer becomes a reality."[5] Alluding to Jesus' clearing of the temple, Jean Danielou writes:

> I have a need
> of such a clearance
> as the Saviour effected in the temple of
>   Jerusalem
> a riddance of the clutter
> of what is secondary
> that blocks the way
> to the all-important central emptiness
> which is filled
> with the presence of God alone.[6]

How do we get this right in practice? By following the example of Jesus.

SUGGESTED READING

☐   Luke 19:45–46

Reflection

Are there ways in which we are in danger of turning God's temple—ourselves and our churches—into a den of robbers?

_____

_____

_____

What practical steps can we take to avoid this temptation?

_____

_____

_____

JESUS' PRACTICE
OF PRAYER

Jesus Prioritizes Time Alone with the Father

Jesus engaged regularly in public worship, but he also prioritized time alone with God as the bedrock from which his public ministry emerged. In Luke 4:42—as in the other Gospels—we see Jesus regularly withdrawing to solitary places for prayer. Jesus placed a premium on time alone with the Father, and his public ministry was an extension of this communion.

We tend to gloss over the account of Jesus' 40 days in the wilderness, viewing the incident as an item unique to Jesus' ministry and irrelevant to our own. In the history of spirituality, however, this account has often been read otherwise. One of the earliest monks, Saint Anthony (AD 251 and the years following), took this phase in Jesus' life as inspiration to head into the desert. He spent the next 20 years ensconced there in an old fort in which he had barricaded himself. Bouyer explains that "it is in order to imitate Jesus in this focal episode in his life that the monk buries himself in the desert."[1]

However, even without such a radical reading of this element in Jesus' narrative, we can plainly construe that extended periods of solitude such as this may not have been atypical in Jesus' piety. The tradition of spirituality insists that such sought-out solitude, whether for half an hour or for 40 days, is vital for spiritual development and renewal. As expressed by Eugene Peterson,

> Solitude alone allows man to discover, and so to face, all the obscure forces that he bears within himself. The man who does not know how to be alone, does not know either (and secretly does not wish to know) what conflicts there are in the depths of his heart, conflicts which he feels that he is incapable of untangling, even of touching. Solitude is a terrible trial, for it serves to crack open and burst apart the shell of our superficial securities. It opens out to us the unknown abyss that we all carry within us. ... [S]olitude discloses the fact that these abysses are haunted: it is not only the depths of our own soul, unknown to us, that we discover, but the obscure powers that are as it were lurking there, whose slaves we must inevitably remain so long as we are not aware of them. In truth, this awareness would destroy us, if it were not illuminated by the light of faith.[2]

The story of Anthony is instructive in another sense: He emerges as more fully human. "The picture that is given us of Anthony as he emerged from his solitude," notes Louis Bouyer, "is ... that of a man

calmed, brought into equilibrium, in whom everything human has become as it were transparent to the
Spirit, docile to his influence."[3] And Henri Nouwen
points out that we learn from Anthony that "we must
be made aware of the call to let our false, compulsive
self be transformed into the new self of Jesus Christ.
It also shows that solitude is the furnace in which this
transformation takes place. Finally, it reveals that it is
from this transformed or converted self that real ministry flows."[4]

All of this may strike us as a bit too medieval.
But before we reject it wholesale, let's reflect on
Nouwen's reference to our busyness, our endless activism, as an indicator of a secular, false self, "which
is fabricated, as Thomas Merton says, by social compulsions."[5] Counterintuitive as the concept may seem
to us, the desert fathers construed busyness as a sign
of laziness! Peterson has this to say of the excessive-
ly busy pastor: "The word *busy* is the symptom not of
commitment but of betrayal. It is not devotion but de-
fection. The adjective *busy* set as a modifier to pastor
should sound to our ears like *adulterous* to character-
ize a wife or *embezzling* to describe a banker. It is an
outrageous scandal, a blasphemous affront."[6]

In the early centuries of the Church, especially around the time of Constantine, some Christians,
sensing the dangers of cultural developments to radical faith, escaped to the desert; hence the designation
desert fathers and mothers. In his little book on sayings of the desert fathers, Thomas Merton describes
how the desert fathers responded to the dangers of
their culture: "they escaped from the sinking ship
and swam for their lives. And the place of salvation is

called desert, the place of solitude."[7] To quote Martyn Lloyd-Jones, someone a long way from the Catholic tradition of spirituality: "You and I ... are what we are when we are alone."[8]

Jesus' extended retreat into the wilderness makes his way crystal clear for us, and he owns it unequivocally. The three temptations are all designed to entice Jesus to avoid the way of the cross; he combats them with Scripture and emerges from the wilderness ready for his public ministry, shadowed throughout, as it will be, by the cross. Comparably, if we are to find our way with integrity and to shed our social compulsions in our narcissistic, consumer culture—a culture that finds any notion of the cross abhorrent—we will need regular times alone with God. If, even in his rural context, Jesus found solitude and silence important, how much more does this apply for us today? In Jean Danielou's words, "The first thing that strikes one is that our technological civilization brings about a change in the rhythm of human existence. There is a speeding up of the tempo which makes it difficult to find the minimum of freedom on which a minimum life of prayer depends."[9]

Ensuring time and space for prayer will often require rigorously rowing against the stream of our culture—swimming for our lives.

Ensuring time and space for prayer will often require rigorously rowing against the stream of our culture—swimming for our lives. But it is precisely as we do so that we will find God in fresh, new, and fecund ways. A Catholic document on the consecrated life rightly notes that

An authentic spiritual life requires that everyone, in all the diverse vocations, regularly dedicate, every day, appropriate times to enter deeply into silent conversation with him by whom they know they are loved, to share their very lives with him and to receive enlightenment to continue on the daily journey. It is an exercise which requires fidelity, because we are constantly being bombarded by the estrangements and excesses which come from today's society, especially from the means of communication. At times fidelity to personal and liturgical prayer will require a true effort not to allow oneself to be swallowed up in frenetic activism. Otherwise it will be impossible to bear fruit.[10]

This will certainly require a daily time of prayer, as well as habitual times of retreat—days and other extended periods away from our daily activity in the interest of being still before the Lord.

Jesus Prays from the Heart

I quoted earlier from Nouwen about the prevalent failure of pastors to pray. He relates this phenomenon to a tendency to intellectualize prayer: "One of these demonic ruses is to make us think of prayer primarily as an activity of the mind that involves above all else our intellectual activities. This prejudice reduces prayer to speaking with God or thinking about God. ... Real prayer comes from the heart."[11]

It seems to me that the Protestant tradition is riddled with examples of this problem. Our spirituality is located far too often in the head, leaving the heart shriveled and drought-stricken, crying out for the rain of God's presence but not knowing how to find it. The charismatic tradition attempts to respond to this problem.

For Jesus, prayer is more than merely thinking about and speaking to God; it is communion emanating from the heart—the center of human existence, as underlined in Old Testament Wisdom literature. This dimension in Jesus' prayer life comes out most clearly in Luke 10 and 11.

> For Jesus, prayer is more than merely thinking about and speaking to God; it is communion emanating from the heart—the center of human existence, as underlined in Old Testament Wisdom literature.

At the end of Luke 10, immediately prior to the Lord's Prayer, we find the story of Jesus' visit to Mary and Martha—an event unique to Luke's account. In this story Mary exemplifies the welcome of Jesus that is appropriate to discipleship. The repetition of "Lord" platforms Jesus' authority, and Mary's position at his feet signifies submission and attentiveness. "The welcome Jesus seeks," notes Green, "is not epitomized in distracted, worrisome domestic performance, but in attending to this guest whose very presence is a disclosure of the divine plan."[12] If we think of prayer as the attitude according to which we, in Merton's words, "wish to hear his word and respond to it with our whole being,"[13] it is appropriate to see in this story instruction about prayer.

The context confirms this impression: Mary's attentiveness to Jesus is followed by Jesus' attentiveness to the Father in prayer. Jesus' Jewish disciples, as we have discussed, have prayed since childhood—no one could accuse them of not knowing the functionality. They have been nurtured in the faith since birth, have confessed their faith, and could take their turn leading in public prayer if called upon to do so. But spending time with Jesus has changed all that. You couldn't hang around Jesus for long without realizing that his life was rooted in a deep, existential, life-giving relationship with the Father. The disciples' prayer times have been formal, never really engaging their lives on the deepest level, but Jesus' are tangibly different—the air of communion with the Father hovers around him like an irresistible fragrance, such that they want it too. Observing something quite new and fresh in Jesus' relationship with the Father evokes their request to be instructed in prayer. "Lord, teach us to pray" is not the request of those who have never encountered the Lord and his purposes; it is the request of disciples in whose hearts a deep desire for the Father has been aroused.

> "Lord, teach us to pray" is not the request of those who have never encountered the Lord and his purposes but that of disciples in whose hearts a deep desire for the Father has been aroused.

Imagine the disciples' delight and wonder when Jesus instructs them, "When you pray, say 'Father.' " Initiating his disciples into prayer from the heart, he uses only a few words, but why should communion with God require many words? We are often confused as to what we are to do with the Lord's Prayer. The entire prayer takes only seconds to repeat—what then?

It is intriguing that the desert fathers advise us to nurture our communion with the Father with short prayers. Again in the words of Nouwen, "Abba Macarius was asked 'How should one pray?' The old man said, 'There is no need at all to make long discourses; it is enough to stretch out one's hand and say, "Lord, as you will and as you know, have mercy." And if the conflict grows fiercer say: "Lord, help." He knows very well what we need and he shows us his mercy.' "[14]

Then there is the marvelous Tolstoy story about three Russian monks on a faraway island. The bishop visits them and is disturbed to discover that they don't know the Lord's Prayer. He devotes all of his time to instructing them in the "Our Father." When he is leaving in his boat, he sees the monks running across the water toward him. "Father," they call out, "we can't remember the 'Our Father.' " Amazed, he asks, "Well, how do you normally pray?" They respond, "Dear God, there are three of you, and there are three of us; have mercy on us!" The bishop, struck by their simplicity and holiness, instructs them to return and be at peace.[15]

Anne Lamott, in her delightful *Traveling Mercies*, reflects that she and her friends, as busy, stressed-out mothers, find themselves continuously mouthing two prayers: "Help, help, help" and "Thank you, thank you, thank you!" The point is that communion facilitated by prayer from the heart requires fewer words, not more words. Words facilitate communion—that is their glory—but in a cerebral culture we expect words to accomplish too much. Jean Vanier reflects:

> To abide or dwell in Jesus is to make our home in him.
> And to let Jesus make his home in us.
> We feel at home with him and in him.
> It is a place of rest for one another and presence to one another.
> It is a place of mutual indwelling and friendship.
> This rest is also a source of life and creativity.
> Abiding in him, we bear fruit, we give life to others.
> We live a mutual indwelling.
> This indwelling is friendship.[16]

Rest, indwelling, friendship—these concepts have their place in such intimacy, but so do the concepts of silence, resting, waiting, soaking, and basking.

SUGGESTED READING

☐ Luke 11:1–13

Reflection

Imagine yourself in the place of one of the disciples observing Jesus pray. What do you notice about him?

_____

_____

_____

How does the Lord's Prayer answer our desire to pray like Jesus?

_____

_____

_____

PRAYER AND MINISTRY

An objection to the emphasis we are developing on prayer is this: Just how do we do this in the context of a busy pastorate, a demanding business life, the treadmill of teaching at a school or university, or the bustle of bringing up young children? In principle, we might agree—absolutely! In practice, maybe not so much.

First, it is worth noting that the pastoral ministry seems to entail a unique commitment to prayer. Like the apostles, the pastoral minister is set apart *for prayer and the Word*, implying that one would, or should, expect the pastor to be more devoted to prayer than Christians in many other vocations. Yet when correctly understood, all vocations are part of the mission of the people of God, and all function to bear witness to God. Witness, like mission, is a holistic concept that includes but should never be reduced to verbal evangelism.

Second, the distinctive emphasis on prayer in the pastoral vocation alerts us that prayer is not merely individual but also communal in nature. I sometimes tell my students that one way to discern whether they have a good pastor is to ask their minister to teach them to pray. The pastor is called to keep the flock attentive to God, and you cannot do this without both modeling and teaching the practice of prayer. Christians characteristically pray when they gather, of course, whether those prayers be of confession, praise, or petition. We have noted the Son's assertion that his Father's house, the temple, is intended as a place of prayer. Jesus' life and death have altered forever the mediating role of the temple so that, in the New Testament, apart from Jesus himself the individual believer (1 Cor 6:19), the congregation (1 Cor 3:16–17), and the Church as a whole (Eph 2:21) are each described as a temple. Minear notes that "the applicability of the image to all three derives from the presence of the Holy Spirit."[1] The Spirit signifies God's presence so that individual Christians, the local congregation, and the larger Church are all places where God is present, where people are in communion with him—and thus where people pray!

> The challenge of balancing prayer with life's other demands is real, but we do well to avoid capitulating to an unspoken premise that prayer has to fit in around the other demands of our busy lives.

Third, it should be noted that there are few ministries as ambitious as that of Jesus. His goal was the redemption of creation, yet his entire ministry is centered on communion with the Father. The challenge of balancing prayer with life's other demands is real, but we do well to avoid capitulating to an unspoken premise that prayer has to fit in around the other demands of our busy lives. Jean Vanier recalls an instance of asking people whether they pray. "Our lives are too busy," they reply. "Well, you must spend a lot of time in prayer, then, when you are on holiday!" Enough said! How ironic to be about our Father's business when we have no time for our Father.

Fourth, we return to Luke's emphasis on successful ministry depending upon prayer; indeed, prayer facilitates successful ministry. The word "successful" should make us uncomfortable, however, because it is too easily defined in terms of numbers: a large, flourishing congregation, a driven church pursuing growth at all costs, etc. By "successful" I refer, in contrast, to ministries that embody the presence of Christ in his world. In the pastorate, that involves a handling of the Word and sacraments that leads to the disclosure of Jesus, with ministry that leads people into union with him and so into participation in the very life of God. In other vocations, witness will be just as real, though likely less direct. A marked characteristic of Luke's Gospel, as we have seen, is its insistence that prayer itself facilitates the disclosure of Jesus.

ILLUMINATION

In our service of Jesus, our great desire is for ministries that are full of him. This, after all, is what the ministry of the Spirit is all about. J. I. Packer tells the story of going to a church intending to preach on the Spirit but being uncertain what illustration to use in his sermon. Rounding a corner, he spots a billboard that is fully illuminated by a spotlight, which is itself invisible. *That*, asserts Packer, is the ministry of the Spirit: to illuminate Jesus so that we are confronted with the enormous reality he is.

In answer to prayer, the Spirit opens us and others to the reality of Jesus; that is what he loves to do. Thus, if we preachers are genuinely concerned about ministering in such a way that Jesus is disclosed to people for who he is, for the sake of our ministry we will make prayer a priority. We will seek to preach and to pastor, as Jesus did, from a life of unceasing prayer. As Peterson asks, "How can I lead people into the quiet place beside the still waters if I am in perpetual motion?"[2] He reflects,

> I want the people who come to worship in my congregation each Sunday to hear the Word of God preached in such a way that they hear its distinctive note of authority as God's Word, and to know that their own lives are being addressed on their own territory. A sound outline and snappy illustrations don't make that happen.
>
> This kind of preaching is a creative act that requires quietness and solitude, concentration and intensity. "All speech that moves men," contends R.E.C. Browne, "was minted when some man's mind was poised and still." I can't do that when I am busy.[3]

In terms of the pastoral ministry, Peterson invokes the image of the harpooner in Melville's *Moby Dick*. The sailors labor fiercely in the whaling boat. But one man in the boat is quiet and poised, waiting. "To insure the greatest efficiency in the dart, the harpooners of this world must start to their feet out of idleness, and not out of toil." Peterson goes on, "It is far more biblical to learn quietness and attentiveness before God than to be overtaken by what John Oman named the twin perils of ministry, 'flurry and worry.' For flurry dissipates energy, and worry constipates it."[4]

Ministry, as Jesus knew only too well, is all about God, and prayer acknowledges this. Elsewhere Peterson urges us to simplify our lives, to resist the compulsive urge to read more and do more: "*The world does not need more of you; it needs more of God.* Your friends do not need more of you; they need more of God. And you don't need more of you; you need more of God."[5]

SUGGESTED READING

☐   Luke 10:38–42

Reflection

Quietly reflect on what gets in the way of your spending time regularly with God.

_____

_____

_____

What changes could you make to become more like Mary?

_____

_____

_____

PRAYING CONTINUALLY

In his final instructions in 1 Thessalonians, Paul exhorts the Thessalonian Christians to "be joyful always, pray continually, give thanks in all circumstances, for this is God's will for you in Christ Jesus" (1 Thess 5:16–18). Many people have been perplexed about this seemingly unfeasible encouragement to pray continually. Commentators on 1 Thessalonians make several suggestions as to what this might mean; it may well, of course, simply be an exhortation to pray regularly. Jean-Louis Chrétien rightly draws attention to the communal dimension of prayer in this respect:

> This interlacing of voices and destinies gave rise to some eloquent considerations in St. Augustine on the perpetuity of prayer. This theme has always aroused debate, for people have wondered how it was possible for an individual to be always praying. The most common solution is to state that any action can become a prayer when it is offered to God, which obviously dissociates

prayer from an act of speech. But there is at least one perpetual vocal prayer, namely that of the community, in which, when one member falls silent, another one takes over and starts to speak. St. Augustine describes the prayer of the Church as the incessant prayer of one single man across space and time. Independently of this theological perspective, the singularity of prayer, which knows that it is one voice in the choir, one moment in a historical community of speech, is clearly emphasized.[1]

It may be that Luke's depiction of Jesus provides some important clues with regard to the continual prayer of the individual believer. Jesus, as we have seen, so dwells in union with the Father that verbal prayer emerges from this deep immersion in communion. In the tradition of Christian spirituality, it is often noted that the goal of our times of prayer should spill over and pervade the whole of our lives. Whether or not this is precisely what Paul had in mind, against the backdrop of Jesus' example it is certainly a desirable goal. Why settle for less when we can be all flame?

RESOURCES FOR FURTHER READING

Chrupcala, L. Daniel. "The Practice of Prayer by Jesus in the Lukan Teachings." Pages 201–236 in *Everyone Will See the Salvation of God: Studies in Lukan Theology*. Studium Biblicum Franciscanum 83. Milano: Edizioni Terra Santa, 2015. This chapter contains a full bibliography of useful sources.

Holmås, Geir Otto. *Prayer and Vindication in Luke-Acts: The Theme of Prayer Within the Legitimating and Edifying Objective of the Lukan Narrative*. Library of NT Studies. London and New York: T&T Clark, 2011.

Longenecker, Richard N., ed. *Into God's Presence: Prayer in the New Testament*. Grand Rapids: Eerdmans, 2002.

Wright, N. T. *The Lord and His Prayer*. Grand Rapids: Eerdmans, 1996.

Readers should note that I have drawn on parts of my book *Introducing Biblical Hermeneutics: A Comprehensive Framework for Hearing God in Scripture* (Grand Rapids: Baker Academic, 2015). I have also drawn from Craig Bartholomew and Robby Holt, "Prayer in/and the Drama of Redemption in Luke: Prayer and Exegetical Performance," in *Reading Luke: Interpretation, Reflection, and Formation*, ed. C. G. Bartholomew, J. B Green, and A. C. Thiselton, Scripture and Hermeneutics Series 6 (Carlisle, PA: Paternoster, 2006; Grand Rapids: Zondervan, 2005), 350–375.

For readers looking for a guide to the practice of prayer, I know of nothing better than *Sacred Space* (Notre Dame: Ave Maria Press). *Sacred Space* is also available online (www.sacredspace.ie).

Important contemporary authors on prayer are Thomas Merton, Eugene Peterson, Kathleen Norris, Jean Vanier, and Henri Nouwen. Peterson has published an annotated list of books on spirituality, titled *Take and Read: Spiritual Reading—An Annotated List* (Grand Rapids: Eerdmans, 1996). The endnotes to this volume also list many useful resources.

NOTES

Chapter 1: Introduction

1. Benedicta Ward, *The Desert Fathers: Sayings of the Early Christian Monks* (London Penguin, 2003), 131.

2. Huffman, D. S., "Luke, Gospel of," in *The Lexham Bible Dictionary*, eds. J. D. Barry et al (Bellingham, WA: Lexham Press, 2012, 2013, 2014, 2015).

3. Saint Athanasius, *On the Incarnation: Saint Athanasius*, Popular Patristics Series Book 44 (Yonkers, NY: St. Vladimir's Seminary Press, 2014), Kindle edition, loc. 56–57.

4. Athanasius, *On the Incarnation*, loc. 720–724.

5. Athanasius, *On the Incarnation*, loc. 859–863.

6. Athanasius, *On the Incarnation*, loc. 865–867.

Chapter 2: The Gospel of Luke as the Story of Jesus

1. Joel B. Green, *The Gospel of Luke* (Grand Rapids: Eerdmans, 1997), 38. Emphasis added.

2. See Brian Richardson, ed., *Narrative Dynamics: Essays on Time, Plot, Closure, and Frames* (Columbus, OH: Ohio State University Press, 2002).

3. But see S. Sheeley, *Narrative Asides in Luke-Acts* (London: Bloomsbury, 2015).

4. This is not to suggest that the historicity of the Gospels is a simple matter, but it is to assert that the effectiveness of the Gospels as speech acts depends upon their historicity and that historical comparisons among the Gospels should follow from, rather than precede, narrative analysis of each Gospel.

5. As Walter Ong's work would remind us, in his significantly oral context Luke would not have wanted to tell a different story but the same story in his own way for his particular audience.

6. "Most excellent" was normally reserved for Roman political officials but may have also been an honorary title; either way, Theophilus was a person of significant status.

7. Green, *The Gospel of Luke*, 10.

8. Green, *The Gospel of Luke*, 47.

9. Green, *The Gospel of Luke*, 47.

10. Green, *The Gospel of Luke*, 34.

11. Green, *The Gospel of Luke*, 50.

12. Green, *The Gospel of Luke*, 51, finds this significant in light of Acts 13:24–5; 18:25; 19:1–4.

13. A verbal form is used in both cases.

14. See David Bosch, *Transforming Mission: Paradigm Shifts in Theology of Mission* (Maryknoll, NY: Orbis, 2003), 108–13. See also J. Massyngberde Ford, *My Enemy Is My Guest: Jesus and Violence in Luke* (Maryknoll, NY: Orbis, 1984), who argues that Luke deliberately heightens messianic expectations in this section so that they can be contrasted with Jesus' controversial approach in Luke 4.

15. Green, *The Gospel of Luke*, 160.

16. Johannes Nissen, *Poverty and Mission: New Testament Perspectives*, IIMO Research Pamphlet 10 (Leiden: Inter-University Institute for Missiological and Ecumenical Research, 1984), 75. See also Joachim Jeremias, *Jesus' Promise to the Nations* (London: SCM, 1958), 41–46.

17. Bosch, *Transforming Mission,* 111.

18. Kenneth E. Bailey, *Poet and Peasant: A Literary-Cultural Approach to the Parables in Luke* (Grand Rapids: Eerdmans, 1976), 83.

19. Green, *The Gospel of Luke*, 697.

20. Green, *The Gospel of Luke*, 24–25.

Chapter 3: The Centrality of Prayer in Jesus' Life and Ministry

1. This expression was probably coined by P. Samain. See L. Daniel Chrupcala, *Everyone Will See the Salvation of God: Studies in Lukan Theology*, Studium Biblicum Franciscanum 83 (Milano: Edizioni Terra Santa, 2015), 201.

2. N. T. Wright, "The Lord's Prayer as a Paradigm for Christian Prayer," in *Into God's Presence: Prayer in the New Testament*, ed. Richard N. Longenecker (Grand Rapids: Eerdmans, 2002), Kindle edition, loc. 1754.

3. Wright, "The Lord's Prayer," loc. 1763–1764.

4. Wright, "The Lord's Prayer," loc. 1953–1957. Readers should note that there is a vast literature on the Lord's Prayer.

5. Green, *The Gospel of Luke*, 434.

6. On the history of interpretation, see Arthur A. Just, *Luke*, Ancient Christian Commentary on Scripture, New Testament III (Downers Grove, IL: InterVarsity Press, 2003), 181–183.

7. Thomas Merton, *Contemplative Prayer* (London: DLT, 1969), 347.

8. Merton, *Contemplative Prayer*, 83.

9. See Just, *Luke*, 182.

10. Søren Kierkegaard, *Works of Love*, trans. Howard and Edna Hong (New York: Harper Perennial, 1962), 169.

11. On this, see especially D. Hamm, "The Tamid Service in Luke-Acts: The Cultic Background behind Luke's Theology of Worship (Luke 1:5–25; 18:9–14; 24:50–53; Acts 3:1; 10:3, 30)," in *Catholic Biblical Quarterly* 65 (2003): 215–231.

12. Jean Vanier, *Drawn into the Mystery of Jesus through the Gospel of John* (Ottawa, ON: Novalis, 2004), 17.

Chapter 4: Prayer and the Story of Redemption in Luke

1. See Paul Blowers, *Drama of the Divine Economy: Creator and Creation in Early Christian Theology and Piety* (Oxford: Oxford University Press, 2012).

2. In Luke 24 Jesus explains the Scriptures to the two traveling disciples as well as the Eleven and others by demonstrating that they all find their fulfillment in him. The specific language attributed to Jesus and the others is important. When Jesus was at the table with Cleopas, his companion, and presumably others, "he took the bread and blessed it (i.e., prayed) ... and their eyes *were opened and they recognized him*." See also D. M. Crump, *Jesus the Intercessor: Prayer and Christology in Luke-Acts* (Grand Rapids: Baker, 1999), 106–108.

3. Compare the question Jesus asks the crowds about their inability to interpret the time (meaning and significance) of Jesus' presence and activity (Luke 12:56).

4. Hamm, "Tamid," 224–226; see also Brown, *Birth*, 280–281.

5. If the Tamid service is the background to Jesus' blessing, then the blessing would refer to Num 6:24–26. See Hamm, "Tamid," 224–226.

6. The opening scene depicts one who has come *from heaven* (Gabriel) to the temple, rendering the providentially designated priest (Zechariah) mute. The closing scene depicts Jesus blessing his disciples as he passes *into heaven*, with the result that they are continually in the temple blessing God. This suggests that Luke is depicting Jesus as the fulfillment of Israel and the temple by portraying him as the priest who can bless and who goes to serve in the reality symbolized by the earthly temple.

7. These bookends confront typical first-century reader expectations, depicting first-century men (particularly a priest and Jesus' disciples) as persons who do not respond properly to God's redemptive action, juxtaposed with first-century women as persons who do. Given their narrative placement, this does not appear inconsequential to Luke's central purposes.

8. Consider the people of Nazareth in Luke 4:16–30; the Pharisees and teachers of Torah tradition in Luke 5:17–26, 30; 6:6–11; 7:36–40; 11:37–54; and the disciples (especially in chapters 9 and 18).

9. Interestingly, when two figures in "dazzling apparel" (24:4) addressed some women, including two women named "Mary" (24:10), concerning the resurrection of Jesus, "they remembered Jesus' words" (24:8). But when they report this, the other disciples are resistant. Likewise, Cleopas and his traveling companion relate these episodes to the resurrected Jesus, whom they do not recognize. But as they tell Jesus about the empty tomb and the report from the women, complete with references to angels (24:22–24), Jesus, not surprisingly, addresses them: "O foolish ones, and slow of heart to believe all that the prophets have spoken!" (24:25). Luke goes out of his way to associate contemplative responses to Jesus with *Marys* who pay attention! Mary, his mother, responds with faith-

fulness when his birth is announced (1:34–38) and carefully ponders words and events concerning her son (2:19, 51). Mary, the sister of Martha, "sat at the Lord's feet and listened to his teaching" (10:39). Finally, the band of women from Galilee, first introduced as a group of providers for Jesus and his disciples (8:1–3), attend to Jesus' death (23:55–56), and when they hear of his resurrection they "[remember] his words" (24:8). Like Anna, these women, who were considered second-class citizens by first-century standards, tune in to God's plan as it unfolds in the life of his Son.

10. Crump, *Intercessor*, 6, responding to problems he perceives with O. G. Harris' important but unpublished PhD dissertation, *Prayer in Luke-Acts: A Study in the Theology of Luke*. Resisting the "cause and effect relationship" proposed by Harris concerning prayer and divine action, which would make prayer "one of the tools through which God is able to act historically," Crump prefers to assert that "prayer is one of the tools through which an individual becomes properly aligned with God's pre-determined action and so is able to participate within God's appointed framework."

Chapter 5: The Acts of the Apostles—Part 2

1. The call of Abraham could serve as a supreme example of this point (Gen 12:1–3).

2. Joel B. Green, "Persevering Together in Prayer: The Significance of Prayer in the Acts of the Apostles," in *Into God's Presence: Prayer in the New Testament*, ed. R. N. Longenecker (Grand Rapids: Eerdmans, 2001), 183–202, 188.

3. Green, "Persevering Together," 194. See also Crump, *Intercessor*, 6, and Peter T. O'Brien, "Prayer in Luke-Acts," *Tyndale Bulletin* 24 (1973): 111–127, 121–127.

4. Joel B. Green, "Persevering Together," 189.

5. For different ways of construing how our prayers relate to the unfolding of God's purposes, compare Crump with John Goldingay, "The Logic of Intercession," *Theology* 99 (1998): 262–270, 266.

6. Consider the answer to the prayer of the gathered believers in Acts 4. Increased boldness came with increased persecution, arrests, threats, and death, not because these things had diminished.

7. Green, "Persevering Together," 193.

8. Likewise, devotion to other basic commitments and resisting God's agenda obscures, for those who fail to see and hear, the good news announced in God's name (Luke 4:16–30; 7:18–35; 8:1–21; 9:51–53; 10:13–24; 11:34–35, 37–53; 12:54–56; 13:10–17; 14:1–6, 25–33; 16:14–17; 18:18–25; 20:19–44; Acts 4:1–22; 5:17–42; 6:8–15; 7:51–8:3; 12:1–5).

9. Green, "Persevering Together," 189–190.

Chapter 6: Prayer and Reading Luke

1. Jean-Louis Chrétien, *Under the Gaze of the Bible* (New York: Fordham University Press, 2015), 44.

2. In general, in both volumes the religious leaders of Israel resist God's redemptive plan. In the first volume the Pharisees and the scribes "knew" Jesus told parables about them but could not respond properly (20:9–19). Jesus castigated the lawyers because they had "taken away the key to knowledge." How? They "did not enter" into the new thing God was doing in and through his servant Jesus (i.e., the kingdom, the new stage of God's drama announced, redefined, and inaugurated by Jesus), and so, implicitly by their negative example and explicitly by their opposition to Jesus, they "hindered those who were entering" (11:52).

3. "Address of Pope John Paul II to Pontifical Biblical Commission (April 23, 1993)," St. Paul Center for Biblical Theology, accessed May 11, 2016, http://archive.salvationhistory.com/ library/scripture/churchandbible/pastoral/pope93.cfm2.htm

4. C. Clifton Black, "Exegesis as Prayer," *Princeton Seminary Bulletin* 23 (2002): 131–145, 138.

5. Black, "Exegesis as Prayer," 139.

6. Black, "Exegesis as Prayer," 143.

7. Joel B. Green, "Learning Theological Interpretation from Luke," in *Reading Luke: Interpretation, and Reflection, Formation*, ed. C. G. Bartholomew, J. B. Green, and A. C. Thiselton (Carlisle, PA: Paternoster, 2006), 66.

8. The parable about the widow and the unjust judge is told to encourage the weak among God's people to pursue justice in a manner driven by hope. Or, better yet, since the widow in the story is the one with whom we are intended to identify, this

parable helps us to view ourselves appropriately as weak servants—unless, of course, we are more like the heartless judge.

9. Numerous papers at least this long could be dedicated to how Luke associates prayer and the Spirit, which, among other things, also informs us concerning the eschatological nature of the drama in which prayer involves us.

10. J. Koenig, *Rediscovering New Testament Prayer: Boldness and Blessing in the Name of Jesus* (San Francisco: Harper, 1992), 11–12.

11. Perhaps disciples of Jesus need to work toward embracing an epistemology of self-abandonment, for to "know" the Father as Jesus did is to relinquish one's life for his purposes and therein to discover what otherwise would be lost.

12. According to Luke 9:46–48, living as children of the Father, as revealed in Jesus, opens up disciples to practices like hospitality and to self-orientations such as meekness. Moreover, the forms this kind of life can take—loving, doing good toward, and blessing enemies and persecutors (6:27–34)—result in emulating and therefore exegeting the Father's character (6:35–36).

13. When he will return all things to his Father (1 Cor 15:20–28).

14. Perhaps the most dangerous temptation, test, or trial remains either the tendency to doubt God's identity as our kind and merciful Father or our own identity as his beloved children (4:3, 9).

15. N. T. Wright, "The Lord's Prayer as a Paradigm of Christian Prayer," in *Into God's Presence: Prayer in the New Testament*, ed. R. N. Longenecker (Grand Rapids: Eerdmans, 2001), 138. See further Wright, "The Lord's Prayer," 137–138, 144–147, for Wright's discussion of the possibility that the "testing" we are prayerfully to avoid is our testing of God, in order that we do not emulate the stiff-necked wilderness generation.

16. One is instantly mindful of Paul's reflection upon these things in Rom 8 and Gal 4, where calling God "Abba" is now a privilege of Gentiles who, recognizing Jesus as Lord, have been confirmed in doing so by the Spirit of promise (see also Wright, "The Lord's Prayer," 151–153). As Jesus taught his disciples about God as their Father ("Your Father knows your needs ... It is your Father's good pleasure to give you the king-

dom," 12:22–32), so the Spirit who searches the deep things of God unveils and clarifies God's radical generosity to his children, "that we might understand the things freely given us by God" (1 Cor 2:12), precisely through the Spirit-empowered proclamation of this same Jesus.

Chapter 7: Prayer and Full-Time Ministry

1. Eugene Peterson, *Working the Angles: The Shape of Pastoral Integrity* (Grand Rapids: Eerdmans, 1987), 2.

2. Peterson, *Working the Angles*, 3–4.

3. Henri Nouwen, *The Way of the Heart* (New York: Ballantine, 1981), 67.

Chapter 8: Why Prayer Must Be Central

1. Alan Storkey, "Postmodernism is Consumption," in *Christ and Consumerism: Critical Reflections on the Spirit of our Age*, ed. C. G. Bartholomew and Karl Möller (Carlisle: Paternoster, 2000), 100.

2. Storkey, "Postmodernism," 115.

3. David F. Wells, *Losing Our Virtue: Why the Church Must Recover Its Moral Vision* (Grand Rapids: Eerdmans, 1999), 80.

4. Peterson, *Working the Angles*, 1.

5. Jean Danielou, *Prayer as a Political Problem* (University of California Press, 1967), 40.

6. Cited in Esther de Waal, *Lost in Wonder: Recovering the Art of Spiritual Attentiveness* (Norich: Canterbury Press, 2003), 19.

Chapter 9: Jesus' Practice of Prayer

1. Louis Bouyer, *A History of Christian Spirituality*, 312.

2. Bouyer, *A History*, 313.

3. Bouyer, *A History*, 319.

4. Nouwen, *The Way of the Heart*, 10.

5. Nouwen, *The Way of the Heart*, 13. See 12–14.

6. Eugene Peterson, *The Contemplative Pastor: Returning to the Art of Spiritual Direction* (Grand Rapids: Eerdmans, 1989), 17.

7. Nouwen, *The Way of the Heart*, 14.

8. Martyn Lloyd-Jones, *Spiritual Depression: Its Causes and Cure* (Grand Rapids: Eerdmans, 1967).

9. Lloyd-Jones, *Spiritual Depression*, 31.

10. *Starting Afresh from Christ: A Renewed Commitment to Conse-crated Life in the Third Millennium* (Sherbrook, QC: Médiaspaul, 2002), 49.

11. Nouwen, *The Way of the Heart*, 68–71.

12. Green, *The Gospel of Luke*, 434.

13. Merton, *Contemplative Prayer*, 83.

14. Nouwen, *The Way of the Heart*, 80.

15. Told in Henri Nouwen, *The Road to Daybreak* (New York: Image, 1988), 50.

16. Vanier, *Drawn into the Mystery*, 272.

Chapter 10: Prayer and Ministry

1. Paul S. Minear, *Images of the Church in the New Testament* (Philadelphia: Westminster, 1960), 77.

2. Peterson, *The Contemplative Pastor*, 19.

3. Peterson, *The Contemplative Pastor*, 21.

4. Peterson, *The Contemplative Pastor*, 25.

5. Eugene Peterson, *Subversive Spirituality* (Grand Rapids: Eerdmans, 1994, 1997), 30.

Chapter 11: Praying Continually

1. Jean-Louis Chrétien, *The Ark of Speech*, trans. Andrew Brown (New York and London: Routledge, 2004), 35.

Printed in the United States
by Baker & Taylor Publisher Services